Remember Your Relations
The Elsie Allen Baskets, Family & Friends

♦♦♦♦♦♦♦♦♦♦♦♦♦♦♦♦♦♦♦♦♦♦♦♦

Elsie Allen (left) and Annie Burke at the Clubhouse, Todd Grove Park, Ukiah, July 13, 1949

"People were curious as to why she [Annie Burke] didn't have any baskets to show... They liked her weaving. They liked her work... So then she got together with my mother [Elsie Allen] and they started holding on to the things they made, plus adding to it... [including] other people's [basketweaving] which has increased the collection. It was really my grandma that got that started."

—Genevieve Allen Aguilar[1]

Remember Your Relations

The Elsie Allen Baskets, Family & Friends

◆◆◆◆◆◆◆◆◆◆◆◆◆◆◆◆◆◆◆◆◆◆◆◆◆

Suzanne Abel-Vidor
Dot Brovarney
Susan Billy

GRACE HUDSON MUSEUM
OAKLAND MUSEUM OF CALIFORNIA
HEYDAY BOOKS, BERKELEY, CALIFORNIA

Co-published by Heyday Books, the Grace Hudson Museum, and the Oakland Museum of California. Please address orders, inquiries, or correspondence to Heyday Books, Box 9145, Berkeley, CA 94709

Publisher's Cataloguing in Publication

Abel-Vidor, Suzanne.
    Remember your relations : the Elsie Allen baskets, family & friends / Suzanne Abel-Vidor, Dot Brovarney, Susan Billy.
    p. cm.
    Includes bibliographical references
    ISBN 0-930588-80-0

    1. Pomo baskets--Exhibitions. 2. Pomo Indians--Basket making. 3. Indians of North America--California--Basket making. 4. Pomo women--Biography.   I. Brovarney, Dot.   II. Billy, Susan.   III. Title.

E99.P65A34 1996   746.41'2'089'975
                                   QBI96-20215

Editing and design: Jeannine Gendar
Production assistance: Wendy Low
Cover design: Jack Myers, DesignSite
Cover photo: Catherine Buchanan.
Photography by Catherine Buchanan and Foley Benson
Cover photo baskets: Top row, left to right, EA #41, 133, 47; Middle row, EA #127, 136, 132; Front row, EA #56, 135, 54, 57; inset, EA #51.

10 9 8 7 6 5 4 3 2 1

Acknowledgments

This catalog is based on the *Remember Your Relations: The Elsie Allen Baskets, Family & Friends* exhibition which we researched and co-curated for the Grace Hudson Museum, City of Ukiah, in 1993. The 1996 presentation of the exhibition at the Oakland Museum of California and the production of this catalog are a collaborative project among the Oakland Museum of California, the Grace Hudson Museum, and Heyday Books.

The exhibit and catalog were developed with the cooperation and support of the Elsie Allen family, especially Genevieve and Ralph Aguilar. We also owe a debt of gratitude to the members of the weavers' families who have generously shared both their memories and personal photographic collections.

The Mendocino County Museum, exhibitor of its own display of the Allen Collection baskets since 1989, was an important resource in the planning of *Remember Your Relations*. Over the past fifteen years, its staff, including Dan Taylor, Sandra Metzler, Mark Rawitsch, Rebecca Snetselaar, Mary Beth Shaw, and Bobbie Yokum, have contributed significantly to the documentation of Pomo basketry in Mendocino County, sharing this information with native peoples, scholars, institutions, and projects such as ours. Individuals who provided invaluable expertise to the research and development of *Remember Your Relations* are: Verle Maize Anderson who, through the recently-formed and rapidly-growing Native American History Project in Ukiah, supplied us with important documentation from the Indian community; Foley Benson who provided assistance and allowed us to use his photographs of the Allen Collection in the index to the collection (see pp. 113–122); Sally McLendon of Hunter College, New York who shared her knowledge of Pomo culture acquired over decades of study; Beverly R. Ortiz who contributed her considerable expertise on basketry technique to this volume; anthropologist Victoria Patterson who provided her time and use of images, from the collection of her late husband, ethnographic photographer Scott M. Patterson; and Sherrie Smith-Ferri whose research on the history of Pomo basketry continues to uncover new information about the lives and traditions of native weavers.

From the outset, Heyday Books publisher Malcolm Margolin enthusiastically embraced the idea of a catalog for this exhibit. Editor Jeannine Gendar bravely tackled the challenge of transforming our diverse collection of text, images, and ideas into a coherent whole. The visual impact of the catalog is a result of Catherine Buchanan's creativity and her mastery of object photography.

Carey Caldwell, Senior Curator of History at the Oakland Museum, recognized the value of *Remember Your Relations* to the expanding scholarship on California's native traditions and arranged to present the show in the San Francisco Bay Area. We owe the successful completion of this publication in large part to Carey and her colleague, Curatorial Assistant Valerie Verzuh, who spent countless hours reviewing material. Both brought to the subject a welcome, fresh perspective and an attention to detail that proved indispensable.

Both the catalog and the Oakland Museum presentation of *Remember Your Relations* have been made possible by generous contributions from the Oakland Museum Women's Board, California Council for the Humanities, LEF Foundation, Oakland Museum History Guild, and the City of Ukiah. We especially would like to thank the many individuals who donated to this collaborative effort, collectively known as Friends of *Remember Your Relations*. The original exhibition at the Grace Hudson Museum was supported by both the City of Ukiah and the Sun House Guild.

Finally, we are indebted to John (1857–1936) and Grace (1865–1937) Hudson whose legacy lives on in the ethnographic and artistic collections of the Grace Hudson Museum.

Suzanne Abel-Vidor
Dot Brovarney
Susan Billy

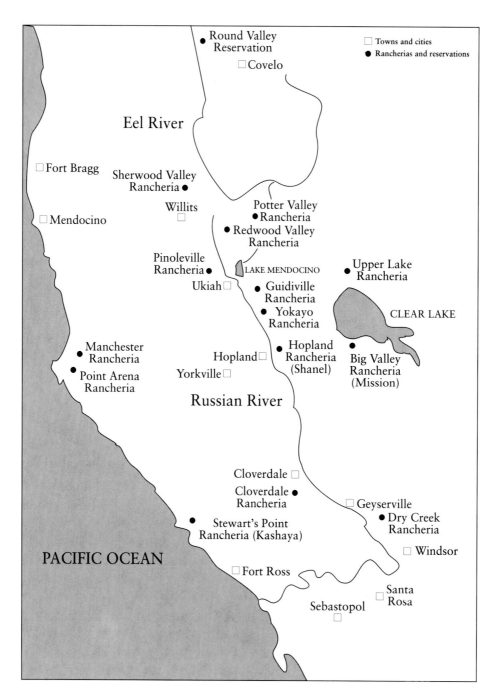

Round Valley
Reservation
□ Covelo

□ Towns and cities
● Rancherias and reservations

Eel River

□ Fort Bragg

Sherwood Valley
Rancheria ●

Willits □

□ Mendocino

Potter Valley
● Rancheria

● Redwood Valley
Rancheria

Pinoleville
Rancheria ●

LAKE MENDOCINO

Upper Lake
● Rancheria

Ukiah □

● Guidiville
Rancheria

CLEAR LAKE

● Yokayo
Rancheria

Manchester
● Rancheria

Hopland □

● Hopland
Rancheria
(Shanel)

●
Big Valley
Rancheria
(Mission)

Point Arena
Rancheria

Yorkville □

Russian River

Cloverdale □

Cloverdale ●
Rancheria

□ Geyserville

● Dry Creek
Rancheria

PACIFIC OCEAN

●
Stewart's Point
Rancheria (Kashaya)

□ Windsor

□ Fort Ross

□ Santa
Rosa

Sebastopol
□

Pomo rancherias (communities) and neighboring towns of Mendocino, Sonoma, and
Lake Counties mentioned in *Remember Your Relations*.

Contents

Introduction

♦♦♦♦♦♦♦♦♦♦♦♦♦♦♦♦♦♦♦♦♦♦♦♦♦

Remember Your Relations: The Elsie Allen Baskets, Family & Friends is about people, cultural identity, and traditions. Although you see objects in these pages, very beautiful ones, neither the catalog nor the exhibition is solely about objects. *Remember Your Relations* is about process: teaching, learning, demonstrating, weaving, creating. It is about choices, too: the choices that Indian people have made for generations and still make today to affirm their identities.

One of the choices made today is whether or not to become a weaver of the beautiful and functional baskets for which the Pomo peoples are justly famous the world over. In every generation since California became a state in 1850—even after the ways of life of Indian people had been altered dramatically and irrevocably—women and men have continued to gather sedge, willow, bulrush, and redbud along watercourses and among the hills of the North Coast. From these natural materials, prepared with consummate skill and care, Pomo weavers always have created baskets of technical and aesthetic virtuosity.

The Elsie Allen Collection has a unique importance among existing collections of Pomo baskets. This assemblage reflects a multigenerational family effort—mother to daughter to granddaughter—to collect and preserve the work of relations, friends, and unknown weavers whose baskets were somehow "special." To date, 26 of the native weavers whose baskets are in the collection have been identified, a remarkably high level of documentation. *Remember Your Relations* focuses on these women, honoring the legacy of their lives and their work.

Elsie Comanche Allen (1899–1990), born in Sonoma County and a longtime resident of Ukiah in Mendocino County, began weaving as a child. It was not until she reached retirement age that she made the choice to devote herself full-time to the practice and teaching of basketweaving. It was a passion she shared with her mother, Annie Ramon Burke (1876–1962), the originator of the Allen Collection, who defied Pomo tradition by asking her daughter to promise not to destroy her baskets when she died. Mrs. Allen also inherited Mrs. Burke's strong sense of personal mission. In a small but important book, *Pomo Basketweaving, A Supreme Art for the Weaver,* Mrs. Allen recalls:

> During the years up to the age of 62, I worked at many jobs... But somewhere within me was the urge to come back to basketmaking. My mother and grandmother worked at basketweaving when I was a child. When I was older I gathered sedge roots, willows, bulrushes and redbud at the same places... with the help of my mother and grandmother we cured the material and made it into baskets. However my grandmother died in 1924, so not only did I lose her help, but most of her examples of baskets as well, as it was customary for an Indian woman to have all her baskets and reeds buried with her.
>
> In the first few years of my married life, I attempted basketweaving. I made a basket of about eight or nine inches and that was buried with my grandmother. My next one-stick coiled basket was buried with my great uncle. A third basket... was buried with my brother-in-law. I didn't have a good feeling about making baskets after that. Mother told me that she wanted me to have her baskets to help me when I started up basketweaving again. So I promised her I would do this... She wanted me to travel and meet people through the baskets and not destroy her baskets and have nothing left for me and others in the future. Mother died in 1962, and I have tried to keep my promise.

Elsie Allen kept her promise by continuing to acquire baskets and by sharing her knowledge and love of weaving with any receptive person, Indian or non-Indian. The legacy begun by Annie Burke

Annie Burke teaches twining to her 6-year-old niece Marie Arnold as part of a demonstration by the Pomo Indian Women's Club at the Museum of Art in the Civic Center, San Francisco, December 1943. Mildred E. Van Every, photographer

Annie Burke, the Pomo Indian Women's Club, and the Creation of a Basket Collection

In 1943 the Pomo Indian Women's Club was asked to put on an exhibition of Pomo basketry at the Museum of Art in the Civic Center of San Francisco. As Elsie Allen, Annie Burke's daughter, recalled:

> When we organized Woman's Club someone asked if we could come down to San Francisco and show baskets and we said "yeah," thinking we have lots of weavers, and find out we don't have lots of baskets.

And this Michael Harrison [former Ukiah Indian Agent] come and give me names in Lake County and Point Arena; and some say "I sold all my baskets" and others just look at me and shut the door in my face... And only one lady, Mrs. John, from Mission, loan us some... And one woman got acquainted with Mrs. Olive Bush—who helped organize Club—and she got excited and arranged to borrow [John and Grace] Hudson baskets and they showed them.

> That's why my mother began making baskets [for her collection]. She said we gonna start showing baskets. She used to foresee things. And every year she showed baskets at the Fair... And she begin to buy baskets from different people.[1]

Three years earlier, on April 6, 1940, Annie Burke, Elsie Allen, Edna Sloan (later Guerrero), Lorraine Lockhart, Myrtle McCoy, and Belle Verriol had presented an exhibition of Pomo baskets at the Saturday Afternoon Club in Ukiah, at which they demonstrated the traditional use and manufacture of the baskets, having mounted a similar exhibition in Lakeport a year earlier.[2]

Al Parsell, an anthropologist and sociologist who attended and photographed the event, found that the exhibition, which brought together prominent women in both the Indian and white communities, "turned out to be a positive step in

Annie Burke (left) and Lorraine Lockhart, members of the Pomo Indian Women's Club, demonstrate the traditional use of Pomo basketry at the Saturday Afternoon Club in Ukiah, c.1940

improving Indian–white relations" in Ukiah.[3]

Annie Burke no doubt noticed the same result. She devoted the rest of her life and a considerable portion of her never large resources to building a personal collection of Pomo baskets specifically to exhibit. Starting with a small group of family baskets of the sort that most native families had, she wove additional baskets and bought still others from weavers then active, paying market prices, despite her own limited income. These she exhibited with her daughter, Elsie Allen, for over a decade at the Mendocino County Fair, the Art Group, and elsewhere. In a two-woman information campaign, they reached out to the public, answering questions, demonstrating the skill and expertise involved in making a Pomo basket, patiently explaining traditional Pomo culture, and generally countering the negative stereotypes and misinformation prevalent about California's native peoples.

It is a remarkable story, and a remarkable collection. It is the only Pomo basket collection known to have been formed by a weaver, especially for educating the public about Pomo people. It is the single largest collection in existence that documents the fine work of a generation of weavers during the period 1940–1965, a time when many authorities have claimed that Pomo basketmaking was extinct. It is almost unique in preserving the name of the maker for most of the baskets. Since most collections of Pomo baskets now in museums are not documented as to maker, we know far too little about the gifted women who produced these strikingly beautiful works of art. Annie Burke's collection, now known as the Elsie Allen Family Collection, thus provides a unique insider's view of a group of fine artists, as selected by a weaver of equal ability and gifts.

—*Sally McLendon*

and Elsie Allen is being carried on by their descendants today. Genevieve Allen Aguilar (b. 1920, Elsie Allen's eldest daughter) is currently custodian of the collection. In 1988, she placed it on long-term loan to the Mendocino County Museum in Willits, Mendocino County.

Mrs. Allen's success in developing a collection of baskets largely documented to weaver is a rare achievement. In most museum and private collections, baskets have lost that essential connection to their creators. By contrast, the contextually rich Allen Collection reflects painstaking efforts by Elsie Allen, researchers, and students to record individual weavers' identities, times of completion, and other important documentary data. This work shows a commitment to educate the public about the Pomo weaving traditions—including the crucial steps of harvesting, curing, and preparing the plant materials needed to make baskets—and to preserve this information for those who will come after.

The woven vessels in the Elsie Allen collection date from the late 19th century into the 1980s, and come in many shapes and sizes. Many are finely coiled in pale sedge, graced with designs in the burnt sienna of split redbud or the coal black of dyed bulrush root. Some are resplendent in brightly colored feathers or glass beads. Others are twined, some loosely, others tightly, their construction determined by traditional functions such as gathering, cooking, parching, or sifting. The largest twined basket is 66 centimeters across; the tiniest coiled piece less than one centimeter. The baskets are from a variety of places: Dry Creek and

Genevieve Aguilar (left) and Elsie Allen showing the family collection at the
Saturday Afternoon Club, Ukiah, c.1940s

"I always said I rode my mother's shirttails because when Mother was invited wherever... she needed company. It was an education for me accompanying her on exhibit displays."—Genevieve Allen Aguilar[4]

Cloverdale in Sonoma County, Upper Lake in Lake County, and a number of rancherias in inland Mendocino County. Of the 131 baskets in the Elsie Allen Collection, over 90 now are documented to 26 Pomo weavers, with about 30 of those attributed to members of Elsie Allen's immediate family.

Following Elsie Allen's lead, we choose to honor the individual women artists without whose creative talent and reverence for tradition this collection would not exist. Documenting each weaver is a challenging and continuing process. This effort is possible because of the assistance of many people, including family, friends, and students of Elsie Allen, staff at regional research institutions, and scholars. With scant written records available on the subject of Pomo weaving and weavers, we relied heavily on consultants and oral histories—the latter largely present-day recollections of the weavers by their relatives and friends and, in the few cases where possible, by the living weavers themselves. Most of these oral histories were recorded by staff of the Mendocino County Museum and Grace Hudson Museum between 1988 and 1993. Both museums contributed information from earlier oral histories, more recent interviews, and other archival records to the exhibition and catalog.

Since 1993, research into the lives of the weavers and their families has continued, yielding additional information and photographs. Names and relationships were clarified further by genealogical research using the recently released 1928 California Indian enrollment records. First-person accounts were drawn from interviews associated with the 1994 film *Pomo Basketweavers: A Tribute to Three Elders.*

Continuing the search to fill in the stories and relationships, further time spent with family was most revealing and rewarding. A coming together for a single purpose emerged. Remembering conversations, events, and relations of long ago triggered cherished memories, helping to connect weavers and families to one another. Old photographs were brought out and shared... answering questions which have no words, touching that place in my heart which longs to know the past. I saw photos of my father as a boy and young man which I had never seen before and images of relatives known to me only by name. For me, it was a highly emotional and moving experience to work on this exhibit and catalog. I feel blessed and fortunate to have been able to participate in such an important project.

—Susan Billy

Further contact with weavers' relatives caused them to delve deeper into family collections. This process stimulated an interest in family history: photographs and stories of family members were seen and shared for the first time, and identities were matched with previously unknown faces and places.

Remember Your Relations reflects a period of brief, though intense, research and remains a work in progress. It provides a glimpse into the life of each weaver documented in the Elsie Allen Collection, her relationships with other weavers, and—wherever possible—her human qualities as remembered by family and friends. We know that many stories are incomplete and that much is left to be told. We take heart, however, that this historical moment is proving a time of cultural revitalization in the Indian community, of renewed public interest in native traditions and in the individuals who have perpetuated those traditions against all the odds.

In recent years, important primary research in archives and museum collections has begun literally to rewrite the history of California to include the voices, values, and creations of many men and women of Indian descent. Like the stories of the weavers in the Elsie Allen Collection, this new inclusive history is still incomplete. We invite those who value this work and can contribute their knowledge to join in the continuing effort to more fully document the lives and timeless gifts of Pomo weavers working in an ancient artistic tradition.

Suzanne Abel-Vidor
Dot Brovarney
Susan Billy

The Pomo People

Before the coming of Europeans, an estimated 11,500 to 21,000 people, now generally grouped together under the name "Pomo," lived in what would become Mendocino, Sonoma, and Lake Counties. They spoke seven related but mutually unintelligible languages, some more different from one another than are the Germanic languages (English, German, Icelandic, Dutch, etc.). Within each of these languages were numerous distinct dialects, particular ways of speaking that identified a person's village or community. These diverse people, who did not in any way think of themselves as a single cultural or political entity, belonged to over seventy politically independent groups—village states, they might be called.

The various Pomo people differed widely in their manner of living. Those who lived along the coast, for example, had shellfish and seaweed almost for the taking. They caught ocean fish, sometimes by casting nets into the sea, sometimes by fishing from rocks with a hook and line. Fashioning rafts out of driftwood, they visited offshore islands to hunt seals and sea lions or gather mussels. They hunted deer and Roosevelt elk in the clearings of the redwood forests, while the bark of the redwood trees provided building materials for their dwellings and fiber for their clothing.

By contrast, the easternmost group of Pomo people lived in several different village communities along the marshy shores and on the islands of Clear Lake. They caught fish in the shallows of the lake and in various tributary streams, using basketry traps, fish weirs, and spears. With bows and specialized arrows, slings, and nets, they hunted the great flocks of geese and ducks that settled into the lake each winter. From nearby quarries they extracted magnesite, from which the most valuable money-beads (later called "Indian gold") were made, and obsidian. From the tule that grew in great profusion everywhere around the lake they created thatch for their dwellings, materials for their clothing, and well-

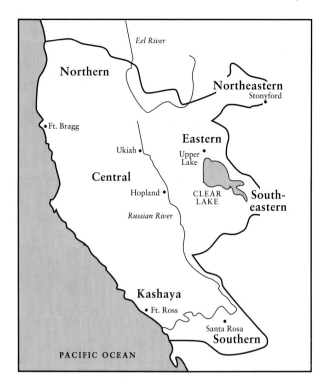

The seven Pomo linguistic groups: Northern, Northeastern, Central, Eastern, Southeastern, Kashaya, and Southern.

trimmed boats with which they crisscrossed the calm waters of their lake.

Between Clear Lake and the coast lived yet other Pomo groups. Their villages dotted the banks of the Russian River as well as parts of the Eel River to the north and Sonoma, Napa, and Petaluma Creeks to the south. This landscape of year-round rivers, valleys studded with oaks, and rolling hills offered a rich habitat, which made this the most densely populated part of Pomo territory. Deer, rabbits, pronghorn antelope, and other game abounded. People also harvested the seeds of some fifteen species of grass, plus a number of berries, greens, roots, and bulbs. Shredded willow bark provided clothing material, and dwelling houses were thatched with grass.

It was in these inland valleys that the largest and most complex village communities could be found. Villages only a few miles apart differed greatly. The village of Kacha, for example, in what is known today as Redwood Valley (just north of Ukiah), consisted of about twelve communal dwellings and perhaps 125 people; it was headed by a single

Elsie Allen and her extended family at the Sturtevant Ranch, Hopland, c.1908. (L-R) Laura Wilbell (aka Billy) and granddaughter Florenda; Mary Jack and baby; Vivian ("Bibb") Burke; Elsie Allen (age 8) and mother, Annie Burke; Dick Burke; Charlie Edwards Jr.; his wife Mow-Sha; Elizabeth Joaquin; Cecilia Joaquin. Bernard Saunders, photographer

"I started working in the hop fields when I was ten years old and during my teens to help add to our family income. This was very hot work during the summer and eventually I decided I wanted to learn something better."—Elsie Allen[5]

chief. Yokaya, in present-day Ukiah, had a population of more than 500, perhaps as many as 1,000. It was headed by a main chief and three subchiefs. Shanel, just to the south of Yokaya, was an enormous village of some 1,500 people. When an early ethnographer, Stephen Powers, examined its ruins in 1877 he identified 104 dwelling-house pits and the foundations of five assembly houses. A village in the immediate vicinity called Shokowa (which may have been another name for Shanel) was also huge, governed by two main hereditary chiefs, an elected war chief, and a number of assembly house chiefs and "speaking" chiefs— some twenty chiefs altogether.

Traditional life among the various Pomo groups was in general characterized by deep knowledge of the land and its resources, and by a long history of restraint in using them, enforced by a clearly articulated legal code, by great technical and artistic skills (basketry, for example), and by strongly held, pervasive religious beliefs. Communities were governed not only by "chiefs," as previously mentioned, but by an elite of

ceremonial leaders, shamans, professional craftsmen, traders, and heads of families. And while we might view each community as an independent village-state, in truth villages were joined to other villages by links of trade, intermarriage, rights to pass, military alliances, reciprocal religious obligations, and yet other ties. While native life has been characterized as "simple," nothing could be further from the truth. The Pomo lived with a number of highly evolved social and cultural institutions, a balanced and sophisticated complexity that gave them stability and a degree of prosperity for many centuries.

The elaborate, carefully constructed world of the Pomo collapsed with the arrival of Europeans. The first to settle in Pomo territory were the Russians who established Fort Ross on the Sonoma coast in 1811. Without much colonial or missionary zest, they had a relatively low impact on Pomo life. The Spaniards founded Mission San Rafael in Marin County in 1817 and Mission San Francisco de Solano in Sonoma six years later, drawing neophytes from the southernmost Pomo groups and causing major disruptions to traditional life. The newcomers also brought dreadful diseases, the cholera epidemic of 1833 and the smallpox epidemic of 1838–39.

With the collapse of the Mission system in 1834, the southern parts of Pomo territory were given over to Mexican land grant holders, and the new overseers widely abused and even enslaved native people. The conquest of California by the United States, the Gold Rush, and the later settlement brought tens of thousands of English-speaking people into what had been Pomo lands, including the northern portions that had largely escaped the incursions of the Russians and the Spaniards. The history of the 1850s and 1860s is one of soul-sickening brutality, as native people were dispossessed, enslaved, hunted down individually, and massacred in groups. During this era reservations were established on the Mendocino Coast and at Round Valley to which many Pomo people were removed. According to the census of 1910, only 1,200 Pomo survived of what had once been a populous, relatively prosperous people.

It is difficult to summarize the various strands of events that have shaped Pomo life since the coming of Europeans. The 1870s "Ghost Dance" move-ment exerted a powerful influence, an influence that is felt to this day. Christian missionaries from a number of denominations moved onto the reser-vations and into Indian communities, with impacts that range from changing traditional forms of wor-ship to introducing schooling and social welfare programs and civil rights advocacy. And during these years a number of individuals have stood out as cultural, political, and religious leaders of some importance.

One important source of strength and continuity came from those few communities that managed to stay close to their original territories during the awful years of the late 19th century. People often lived more or less as squatters on the land of a sympathetic white rancher or farmer, who would generally use them as a source of cheap labor. From here they ventured out to pick fruit or hops, to work in the grain fields, to cut wood, or to do

domestic work for surrounding ranchers. In many ways these small communities served as cultural centers of Pomo ways. In some of them people pooled their money to buy their own land, and some of the lands they purchased prospered as farming communities. It was from communities such as these that many of the leaders and much of the activism of later years arose.

Today there are some seventeen small reservations or rancherias in Sonoma, Mendocino, and Lake Counties, some of which the Pomo share with neighboring people. Many more Indians live off the reservation, some in rural areas, others in cities like Santa Rosa, Ukiah, or Sebastopol. Still others live further away, in San Francisco, Sacramento, or Los Angeles, but maintain ties to their communities by returning home for dances, ceremonies, or simply to visit.

The last several years have witnessed dramatic losses as well as substantial gains for the Indian community. The losses have generally involved the passing of an older generation, those who had a deep understanding of traditional ways and a thorough knowledge of language. Some of the seven Pomo languages are virtually extinct, others—once the repository of a huge body of song, poetry, a manner of thinking, a unique wisdom—have been reduced to a handful of elderly speakers.

There have also been gains, and these have been real and encouraging. While Indian people are still poor, badly housed, and deficient in health care compared to the general population, things have at least improved during the last decades. And the last ten years have also witnessed something of a cultural renaissance as a younger generation has taken a new interest in the songs, dances, ceremonies, languages, and arts of their people.

The huge distinctions that once separated the many Pomo communities from one another have not disappeared, but as time passes they seem to be fading. Today, people seem more comfortable with the identity of "Pomo" than ever before, suggesting not only of a sense of shared history but perhaps a shared future as well.   —*Malcolm Margolin*

Pomo Basketry: An Introduction

The Pomo and Their Baskets

Pomo baskets have become recognized throughout the world for their beauty, quality of construction, elaborate designs, and sumptuous ornamentation of beads and feathers. Pomo baskets also stand out due to their diverse range of techniques and forms. Pomo weavers produced both coiled and twined baskets in relatively equal numbers. In contrast, other North American Indian peoples produced either predominantly coiled or predominantly twined baskets. Just as the various Pomo tribes showed cultural similarities and differences, so too did their basketry. While Pomo baskets exhibit general similarities in construction techniques, form, function, and materials used, they also show regional variation. Some of these variations result from geographical availability of plant resources. Coastal weavers, for instance, tended to use bracken fern for their black patterns, while inland weavers used bulrush root. These variations also resulted from divergent aesthetic and technical choices.[6]

Because of their range, the baskets produced by a given Pomo tribe sometimes had more in common with those of their non-Pomo neighbors—members of bordering Yuki, Patwin, Lake Miwok, Wappo, and Coast Miwok tribes—than with those of other Pomo tribes. In fact, some Pomo village communities produced baskets indistinguishable from those made by non-Pomo village communities.

Aesthetics and function governed the choice of basketry materials, the basket's shape and size, and the weaving techniques used. The methods used to start and end particular types of baskets, place design and decorative elements, and splice new sewing strands all combined in distinctive ways among various Pomo groups. Within the limits of such weaving rules, each individual basketmaker had a personal style which showed through, a style recognizable to people who knew her or his work well.

Basketry Types and Techniques

While they may be viewed as art pieces because of their exquisite appearance, many Pomo baskets were tools for commonplace, utilitarian tasks. Others served as gifts that fulfilled certain social and economic obligations.

Women gathered, stored, processed, cooked, and served food in baskets. Men trapped fish, quail, woodpeckers, and other animals in baskets. Baskets were containers for transporting wood and other items. They cradled babies. Small-sized baby baskets with dolls inside served as girls' toys, as did miniature burden and mortar baskets. As gifts, baskets provided a way to commemorate special occasions, such as weddings and funerals, and to redistribute wealth. Special elliptical "boat" or "canoe" baskets held valuable items, such as shell and magnesite beads. Pomo doctors used baskets as part of their healing practices; Pomo prophets, seers, and revelators used them in ceremonies. During certain sacred dances, Pomo dancers wore elaborately feathered headpieces fabricated on basketry foundations.[7]

The time needed to complete any given basket varies according to its size, fineness of stitching, the technique used, and the effort needed to prepare materials. Whereas an unpeeled whole shoot openwork woodpecker trap could be woven in less than an hour, a watertight cooking basket could take months to complete.[8]

Pomo weavers used a range of techniques to create their baskets. Seedbeaters were fashioned with a one-strand, plain weft (wickerwork) technique,[9] and baby cradles by lashing stout dogwood or hazel shoots together with string, using a sort of double half hitch.[10] All other Pomo baskets used variations of two basic weaving techniques—twining and coiling.

Weavers created most of their utilitarian baskets with twining, an older style of basketmaking than coiling. Twining involved a type of finger weaving in which the maker manipulated two or three horizontally arranged sewing strands (weft) around a base of vertically arranged shoots (warp). There

These twined and coiled baskets by multiple weavers illustrate the wide range of functional basketry associated with the Pomo: (L-R, Rear: Annie Burke or Maude Scott, acorn cooking basket, n.d. EA#42; unidentified weaver, burden basket, pre-1884 EA#44; Middle: Frank Miller's aunt, pepperwood nut basket, n.d. EA#20; Mrs. Kyman, mortar hopper, n.d. EA#33; attributed to Laura Wilbell, serving basket, n.d. EA# 37; unidentified weaver, winnowing basket, n.d. EA#126; Front: unidentified weaver, fish trap, n.d. EA#95; Susie Santiago Billy, gift basket, n.d. EA#130; unidentified weaver, canoe gift basket, n.d. EA#73; Annie Burke, gift basket, 1940 EA#134; unidentified weaver, coiled basket, n.d. EA#48)

were six basic styles of twining in Pomo weaving: (1) two-strand, plain weft twining (also called plain twining, simple twining, or *bamtush*); (2) two-strand, alternate pairs twining (also called diagonal twining, twill twining, or *chuset*); (3) two-strand, full-turn twining (also called wrapped twining, lattice bound weave, or *lit*), which was used in combination with alternate pairs twining or, more rarely, plain weft twining to create design areas; (4) lattice twining (also called *ti* weave); (5) three-strand braiding; and (6) three-strand twining. Unlike standard twining, in which two active weft elements successively engaged perpendicular passive warp elements, in full-turn twining only one element moved over the surface, while the other was floated.[11]

Unlike that of other native groups, Pomo twined basketry typically employed multiple twining techniques in the same basket, both for aesthetic and functional purposes.[12] For example, weavers often combined diagonal twining with lattice twining. The horizontal rods added during lattice twining reinforced the basket in crucial places subject to extraordinary wear.

Oak woodland above Vichy Springs, Mendocino County, October 31, 1982.
Scott M. Patterson, photographer

"The typical inland valley environment, home to pepperwood, buckeye, oaks, redbud, elderberry, Indian potato plants, clover, deer, squirrels, quail, doves, people and much else of beauty and usefulness."—Victoria Patterson[14]

Pomo weavers typically coiled gift and commercial baskets. The most intricate Pomo coiled work had upwards of 80 stitches to the horizontal inch.[13] The inner core of Pomo coiled baskets consisted of a foundation made from one or three rods, commonly willow, but also fashioned from other basketry material. When coiling, basketmakers used a sharp, tapered awl to pierce a hole between the rods in their one-rod coiled baskets, or through the top rod in their three-rod work. Then they pulled a sewing strand through that hole. The stitching spiraled in a counterclockwise fashion outward from the basket's start. Except for boat baskets, Pomo weavers generally started coiling around various styles of knots, although beads and buttons also served the purpose.[15]

The diversity of Pomo techniques allowed for an unusually wide range of basketry shapes, each suited to its particular function. Such shapes included cones, ellipses, spheres, and basins, with varied gradations and combinations of the same.[16]

The range of techniques also accommodated a variety of color designs, from the straightforward to the complex. Such designs consisted of a single color, either red, dark brown, or black, against a tan background.[17] The fancier twined work—close-twined with evenly sized sewing strands—had intricate designs. Horizontally banded designs predominated on three-strand twined baskets, plain twined baskets, and lattice twined baskets. Diagonally twined baskets generally had diagonal designs or diagonally crossing patterns.

The widest range of design possibilities occured on coiled work, which offered the greatest flexibility in their placement. Like twined baskets, coiled baskets had horizontal banding, diagonal, and crossing designs. They also had vertical and freeform designs.[18]

The oldest Pomo baskets in collections had geometric design elements, such as triangles, diamonds, rectangles, lines, and zigzags. Some of these elements represented natural objects, like plants and animals. Others represented artifacts, such as arrowheads. Still others had no particular meaning.[19] Some basket designs had very personal meanings. Kathleen Smith recalls that her Mih·ila'kʰawna Pomo grandmother, Rosa Bill Lozinto, wove a 15-inch long boat basket with a triangular design. The design represented her eight living children.[20]

Women and Men as Weavers

Both women and men wove Pomo baskets. Men specialized in making twined, openwork baskets used for traps and carrying wood. These had an up-to-the-right slant to the sewing strands (weft). Not only did traps accord with the traditional hunting roles of men, but such baskets, which used whole, often unpeeled shoots, required greater hand strength to create than coiled baskets and other, more delicate twined forms fashioned from finer materials. Men also made baby baskets. Women specialized in coiled baskets and the fancier twined ware. In contrast to the twining methods used by men, women wove their twined pieces with a down-to-the-right slant to the weft.[21]

Typically, basketmakers specialized in a few techniques, trading for or purchasing those types

they did not make, but needed. However, exceptionally talented individuals like Mary and William Benson could and did make baskets using the full range of techniques.[22]

Materials

Pomo weavers had access to a variety of strong and flexible materials. This was certainly a factor in the high quality of the baskets themselves.[23] Materials included: (1) sedge rhizomes (underground runners) or "white root," used for sewing strands and knotted coiled starts (*Carex barbarae, C. obnupta,* and others); (2) willow shoots, used for the warp and weft in twined work and the foundation in coiled work (*Salix hindsiana, S. laevigata*); (3) willow roots, used for foundation in some miniature coiled baskets and for binding rim sticks (*Salix* spp.); (4) creek dogwood and hazel shoots, valued for making baby baskets (*Cornus glabrata* and *Corylus cornuta* var. *californica*); (5) oak, used for hopper mortar, burden basket, and baby basket rim sticks (*Quercus* spp.); and (6) grey pine root, used as weft in large twined pieces (*Pinus sabiniana*). For designs: (1) bulrush rhizomes or "black root" (*Scirpus* spp.); (2) redbud shoots (*Cercis occidentalis*); and (3) bracken fern rhizomes (*Pteridium aquilinum* var. *pubescens*).[24] In modern times imported chair cane became a popular foundation material in coiled baskets due to its evenness and lack of larval damage, a common occurrence in willow. While it is not as dense and strong as willow, dogwood, and hazel, some contemporary baby basket makers also use it, particularly in their miniatures.[25]

Decorative elements added to Pomo baskets included clamshell disk beads, magnesite beads, and glass trade beads. Pomo baskets are probably most famous, however, for the beautifully colored and iridescent feathers incorporated into them, including: quail topknots (black); meadowlark breast feathers (yellow); mallard neck and head feathers (green); acorn woodpecker head feathers (red); and bluebird and jay breast feathers (blue).[26] These feathers sometimes covered the entire surface of the basket in velvety, multi-hued patterns. On other baskets they protruded periodically in tufts of red feathers or black topknots, incorporating color and texture into the woven design.

As with all other aspects of Pomo life, gathering required restraint and patience. Weavers could/can only harvest each basketry plant at certain times of the year. They used specialized burning techniques, and still use specialized digging and pruning techniques to insure the quality of their materials and gathering areas.[27]

Except for unpeeled, whole shoots used in openwork baskets, basketmakers need to store their materials prior to use. This curing process, which can continue for one, two, or more years, allows the plants' water content to evaporate away, thereby insuring that the basket will maintain a tight, even weave.[28]

Shortly after gathering, while their materials are still fresh, basketmakers begin preparing what they have gathered for eventual use in their baskets. For example, they split their sedge and strip the bark away, and they strip or scrape the bark from their foundation rods.[29]

To achieve the desired dark brown or black hue for bulrush and bracken fern, weavers dyed them in mud mixed with ash or, in more modern times, in a slurry of rusted iron, black walnut, tea leaves, coffee grounds, and/or acorn.[30]

After curing them, basketmakers scrape their foundation rods to an even diameter. They soak their split material until it is flexible, then carefully trim each strand to the same width and an even thickness. Many weavers consider this painstaking work to be the hardest part of making a basket.[31]

Rules

> We take from the earth and say please. We give back to the earth and say thank you.
> —Julia Parker[32]

Besides mastering largely technical processes, Pomo weavers adhered to special rules which affirmed their place in the world and acknowledged their responsibility to the plants and to each other. For example, they did not work on their baskets when they felt unhappy. Some weavers fasted the night before gathering, and they always prayed before harvesting any materials. As a way of thanking the Creator and the plants, weavers gave offerings of such items as beads, food, and money. They did not gather when they were menstruating, nor did they usually weave when menstruating. To do so, they said, could result in such consequences as arthritis, blindness, and "ill luck."[33] In some areas women wove flicker quills into their baskets if their menstrual cycle began while they were weaving.[34] Some Pomo basketmakers purposely wove pattern variations or breaks, called *daus,* into their work to provide an opening for the basket spirit to use when inspecting the basket.[35]

The Commercial Market

A commercial market developed for Pomo and other North American Indian baskets in the late 1880s, and persisted into the 1930s. When visualizing Pomo baskets, most people think of the finely woven baskets produced for this commercial market. This style of work may best be termed "art baskets." Weavers produced such work as objects of aesthetic value, not for functional use.[36]

The market provided a number of native women with the opportunity to make money at a time when there weren't many occupations available to them, other than low-paying laborer jobs. By the time the market developed, Pomo individuals no longer needed to create twined, utilitarian ware for use around the house because inexpensive, manufactured substitutes were widely available. Freed from functional constraints, weavers creatively responded to the market by producing increasingly finer and more dramatic work. While some museums still sought twined ware for type collections, the general decline in demand for this style resulted in fewer men making baskets. Some men, like William Benson, spurred by the commercial possibilities, turned to making the same type of fine coiled work women were making. Commercial weavers experimented with new designs, such as human forms. They wove tiny, multicolored glass beads across the entire surface of their baskets. With encouragement from their buyers, basketmakers competed to use finer and finer stitches. They also made smaller and smaller baskets, some tinier than the head of a pin. These microminiature baskets were a novelty item produced for the market. They were popular with buyers, who used them as watch fobs, charms, and conversation pieces. Other innovations included new shapes, like goblets and plaques.[37]

Innovations also included the creation of unusually large baskets. At the behest of her husband, one enterprising weaver, Mary Smith, began making a gigantic basket for display at the 1916 Panama-Pacific Exposition in San Francisco. She died before finishing the basket, but ten other weavers completed it. An eleventh woman gathered materials. The basket, some four feet wide and nearly 18 inches tall, is the largest Pomo coiled basket in existence.[38]

After the market for baskets collapsed in the thirties, fewer Pomo individuals wove baskets. As native women started working in a variety of other occupations, they had less time for basketmaking. For some, basketry was such an enjoyable and important part of their lives that they would not think of stopping.

To insure that Pomo basketry would continue into the future, some women, including Elsie Allen, broke long-standing traditions.

> Elsie wrote a book about how to weave Pomo baskets. That was the first time I had ever heard of a Pomo weaver breaking the tradition of only teaching your relatives how to weave. Elsie felt that if she didn't share what she knew, it would die. She didn't want that to happen, so she broke the tradition. She got a lot of flack, but the time was right for people to listen to her.[39]—Kathleen Smith

Changing laws spurred additional innovation. Elsie Allen told her student Marion Steinbach[40] that she started using pheasant feathers in her baskets after "government people," most likely Fish and Game officers, confiscated some baskets due to laws restricting possession of most bird feathers. Elsie hid her baskets to prevent their confiscation. Because pheasant feathers were legal to possess, Elsie began to use them in her baskets. When ill

health prevented her from weaving in the eighties, she gave her pheasant feathers to Laura Somersal, who then began to use them in her own baskets.[41]

Pomo Basketry Today

Pomo elders have passed the skill of basketry on to a new generation of basketmakers, Indian—of both Pomo and non-Pomo heritage—and non-Indian alike. While most of this new generation is female, some are male. Most weave infrequently, and all specialize in particular types of baskets, most commonly small coiled pieces and baby baskets, both miniature and full-sized.

Contemporary Pomo basketmakers are faced with difficult barriers to the practice of their skill. Of tremendous concern is the difficulty of finding the time to make baskets while juggling family, work, and school responsibilities. Access to materials is the other major problem. Many traditional gathering sites have been destroyed by development activities. Private property restrictions have further limited access. Weavers have few secure gathering sites, whether on private or public lands, and some areas have become contaminated with strangers' waste and refuse.[42] While such destruction and restrictions are by no means new phenomena (see, for instance, Mason 1902:452),[43] the pace of that destruction has increased, and Pomo basketmakers must often travel long distances to gather their materials.

In some cases weavers have taken extraordinary measures to protect gathering areas. In the 1970s, for instance, several Pomo weavers, including Elsie Allen, collaborated with non-Indians to transplant sedge from an area slated to be flooded by the Warm Springs Dam to a protected plot outside the area of inundation.[44]

While history has placed barriers ahead of today's Pomo weavers, those who continue to weave have the patience, skill, and determination to carry Pomo basketry into the future.[45]

—Beverly R. Ortiz

Elsie Allen holds a stunning basket (EA#41) made by her mother, master weaver Annie Burke. Santa Rosa, 1986. Dugan Aguilar, photographer

"Basketweaving needs dedication and interest and increasing skill and knowledge; it needs feeling and love and honor for the great weavers of the past who showed us the way. If you can rouse in yourself this interest, feeling and dedication, you also can create matchless beauty and help me renew something that should never be lost." —Elsie Allen[1]

Elsie Comanche Allen

(1899–1990)

◆◆◆◆◆◆◆◆◆◆◆◆◆◆◆◆◆◆◆◆◆◆◆◆

Elsie Comanche Allen was born near Santa Rosa to Annie Ramon and George Gomachu (anglicized to Comanche), but she spent her earliest years with her maternal grandmother, Mary Arnold, near Cloverdale. In her autobiographical book, *Pomo Basketweaving: A Supreme Art for the Weaver*, she described this "rather isolated" but idyllic existence:

> Rocks and leaves served well to build houses and make doll people... Elderberry bushes, willows and other trees were named as persons and given a personality in my imagination... I would run through the animal trails in the chamise brush with my mother's fox terrier... He was as happy as I to have a playmate and was a favorite pet along with a kitty I treasured... [2]

Her widowed mother's second marriage, to Richard Burke (c.1907), took Elsie Allen's family to the area surrounding the village of Hopland, in southern Mendocino County. They lived in a wooden house in the winter and by the Russian River in a traditional Pomo summer house of willow when the heat came.

> In the summer we moved down by the river and built a kind of a hut like our people had in the old days, a house made of leaves put over willow frames. We cut the willows down and wove them over posts, then covered this with leaves. The roof of our house was made from willow branches set across the roof top and smaller willow twigs were woven in and out to form a solid roof to keep the hot sun out. [3]

It was during these summers that Elsie joined her relatives in seasonal hop picking for growers on several large ranches around Hopland. Here, from the elders in her extended family, she learned to speak Central Pomo as fluently as her native Southern Pomo. She learned other traditional skills in Hopland—hunting and fishing, and gathering and preparing wild plants for food and to use in basketweaving. From these experiences, Elsie Allen formed a belief, carried throughout her life, that tradition was important, but could be blended successfully with newer ways. She recalled:

> We bought flour and sugar and other items from the store and used a wood stove to cook upon, which I preferred to the old ways of my grandmother, who cooked by an open fire such foods as ground acorns, pinole, deer meat and fish, and other gathered foods. [4]

At the age of eleven Elsie Comanche, like so many other Indian children of that era, was sent to a federal boarding school at the Round Valley Reservation near Covelo, in northeastern Mendocino County—

Elsie Allen, miniature baskets (L–R, Rear: EA#71, 114; Middle: EA# 108, 112; Front: EA#111, 109).

Pomo miniature baskets were not made traditionally; they were a response to market demand, beginning in the 1890s, by collectors for all kinds of native-made basketry.

"It's harder to make a small basket. Miniature baskets are made to show the weaver's dexterity and skill."
—Susan Billy[5]

far from family and home. At these boarding schools, teachers punished students for "talking Indian," believing such treatment would transform Indian children into fully assimilated Americans. Beatings she received for speaking her language convinced Elsie Allen never to submit her own children to the risk of such mindless abuse. More than fifty years later, she described the decision she and her husband made to speak only English in their home:

> When our children were young we were so sure that only English would be of use to them in later life that most of the time we talked only English in front of them... Now we are not so sure and are beginning to feel it is sad they did not learn their own native tongue.[6]

After a year, her mother decided that Elsie would not return to the Covelo school. The next year, when she was thirteen, Elsie attended the new Hopland Indian School on the nearby rancheria. She spoke of her three years there very positively, saying that she "finally began to learn to read, write, and talk English."

As a teenager Elsie learned to weave baskets. Elsie Allen's primary teachers were her mother, Annie Ramon Burke, and her maternal grandmother, Mary Arnold, both of whom learned traditional weaving skills from Elsie's great-grandmother Gunsissie (c.1820–1905), also known as Fannie or Concepcion. Annie Burke, who spent countless hours weaving baskets, instructed her daughter in techniques for gathering, drying, preparing, and weaving basketry materials, and inspired in her a boundless pride in the tradition of Pomo basketmaking.

At eighteen, Elsie Comanche—tired of the hard and often dull labor of the hop fields and curious about the world—ventured to San Francisco, where she worked for about nine months before becoming ill with the virulent flu of 1918. Sent back home to Hopland by her employers at St. Joseph's Hospital, Elsie eventually recovered on a traditional diet of acorn mush, the only food her stomach would tolerate.

In 1919, Elsie Comanche married Arthur Allen in both a Catholic ceremony and a separate Indian ceremony at which the families exchanged traditional gifts. They settled at Pinoleville Rancheria just north of Ukiah and raised a family of four children: Genevieve, born in 1920; Leonard, in 1922; Dorothy, in 1924; and George, in 1928.

Marriage, raising four children, and working at a variety of jobs left Elsie Allen little time to engage in the labor-intensive and exacting

Elsie Allen in multiple strands of clamshell disk beads, outside her home, c.1970. Once a trade item similiar to money, clamshell disk beads are still highly prized as objects of personal adornment and decoration on gift baskets.

Elsie Allen, gift basket, 1977 (EA#80)
also pictured at right, below.

*"[Laura Somersal] didn't use
pheasant feathers until the later
years. She used woodpecker,
California quail, and some other
native birds [like] the mallard with
their pretty green feathers. But Elsie
Allen used the pheasant feathers.
But then when Elsie couldn't make
baskets any more, she had a very
large collection of pheasant feathers
that she gave to Auntie [Laura]."*
—Bette Holmes[7]

practice of basketweaving. She lost one of her two primary teachers when her grandmother Mary Arnold died in 1924. Mrs. Allen recalled in her autobiography that although she did weave some baskets in the early years of her marriage, they were buried with family members. "I didn't have a good feeling about making baskets after that," she said.

Annie Burke also became unhappy with this tradition that dictated the continual loss of material heritage. Recognizing that the demands of a young family and her daughter's disaffection with weaving would pass over the years, she told Elsie that her baskets should not be destroyed when she died; Elsie would need them when she took up weaving again. Mrs. Burke also saw the baskets as a way to preserve a valuable part of Pomo culture and to communicate its significance to the wider world. She wanted her daughter to follow her example, to go out and display the family baskets, to explain to people how they were made, and to teach people to appreciate them.

At the age of 50, Mrs. Allen made a conscious choice to share her love and knowledge of Pomo basketry. She tells the story of that moment in her autobiography:

> My daughter [Genevieve] visited me and wanted me to go with her to a Chinese restaurant where I expected to see none but Chinese eating. I was amazed to see other races eating there and saw also how proud the Chinese were of their heritage. Since I felt that the Pomos were one of the greatest basket weavers in the world, I resolved in my heart that this wonderful art should not be lost and that I would learn it well and teach others.[8]

In 1961, the year before her mother's death and nearly forty years after her grandmother's death, Elsie Allen returned to basketmaking, nearly full-time. For the next thirty years, she gathered materials, wove, exhibited her work, and collected the work of other artists. She consulted for museums, anthropologists, and linguists, which took her far and wide: to Berkeley, San Francisco, Chicago, New York, and Washington, D.C. She taught basketweaving to Indian and non-Indian students.

One of her students, the late Marion Steinbach, worked with Elsie for over twenty years and left an important record of their relationship in the form of notes, letters, slides, samples of plant materials, and illustrations of technique. Another was Elsie Allen's grandniece, Susan Billy, who carries on the tradition of weaving, teaching, and consulting.

Elsie Allen demonstrates at the 12th District Fair, Ukiah, 1960s. Roy Scammon, photographer

"As a senior citizen, she was driving to San Francisco doing seminars at the age of 70. She was never home. She was... kind of a basketweaving social butterfly, if you will, in terms of really going wherever the need or desire was to learn."
—Linda Aguilar McGill[9]

Below: Elsie Allen, three gift baskets, one coiled basket, and one work basket (L-R: EA# 80, 54, 2, 78, 72)

"Elsie was totally at ease weaving the full range of techniques."
—Susan Billy[10]

Elsie Allen, Pomo basketmaker, 1981. Scott M. Patterson, photographer

"The day Scott came to take the photo of Elsie, he told her to bring out the basket she was working on. But when she sat down with all these baskets around her, the coiled basket she brought out was too small to show through the camera's eye, so he asked her if she had anything larger that was unfinished. She laughed and grabbed my 'thousand stick' and Scott liked the effect. Elsie told me that's why she was laughing in the photo."—Susan Billy[11]

Elsie Allen and Susan Billy at the Allen home, 1981. *Ukiah Daily Journal* photograph

"Always when I was with her, that was the impression I had—she brought to each moment, her whole life. It was like reaching back, where she came from; it came through to who she was in that moment... you could see her formulating what it was she was trying to say... through all of her experience. Anything she said was greater than the words themselves."—Susan Billy[12]

Elsie Allen teaches docents at the Sun House, now a part of the Grace Hudson Museum, Ukiah, 1979

"Since I felt that the Pomos were one of the greatest basket weavers in the world, I resolved in my heart that this wonderful art should not be lost and that I would learn it well and teach others."—Elsie Allen[13]

Annie Burke, work baskets, storage baskets, and canoe basket (clockwise from back, left: EA #10, 75, 22, 132, 41)

"My mother weaved all type baskets, twine, three-willow, one-willow, small... My mother started weaving a smaller basket when people came around and wanted to buy baskets. You had to make smaller baskets to finish right away. The big baskets took a long time."—Elsie Allen[1]

Immediate Family

♦♦♦♦♦♦♦♦♦♦♦♦♦♦♦♦♦♦♦♦♦♦♦

It is a sacred thing to be entrusted with old knowledge, though often, when the teaching has been uninterrupted from generation to generation, this oral tradition and work of hands is simply viewed as a natural part of life. As Pomo lifestyle and existence began to change dramatically in the late 1800s and early 1900s, the people adapted. Sometimes this was very painful and sometimes the transition was accepted and embraced. Some could see life must change. As grandmothers, aunties, and mothers continued to pass the basketry traditions to grand-daughters, nieces, and daughters, times were changing. No longer did each woman feel the need to weave baskets. After all, now there were pots and pans, boxes and cupboards, suitcases, jobs. Some women began to leave the home for work. Others continued to weave. Some did both.—Susan Billy

When Elsie Allen was born in 1899, she entered a Pomo world in transition. Her great-grandmother, her grandmother, and other • relatives of their generations had lived through the most intense period of white settlement in Pomo territory. The decades following the 1850s were filled with massive loss and continual adaptation. By the time of Elsie's birth, many weavers were selling their baskets to enthusiastic white collectors. Modern products were quickly replacing baskets for cooking, storage, and other traditional uses. Nonetheless, some Pomo women continued to use baskets, and despite fifty years of adaptation to white culture, they continued to practice and teach the ancient weaving tradition they had learned from their foremothers. The key to the endurance of Pomo basketweaving is family. The creative work of Elsie Allen and eight family members comprises more than one third of the identified baskets in the Allen Collection.

Elsie Allen learned basketweaving primarily from her mother, Annie Burke, and her maternal grandmother, Mary Arnold. Elsie's family included her older half-sister, Agnes Commache, and Agnes' grandmother, Mrs. Kyman. After the death of her first husband, George Gomachu, Elsie's mother married Richard Burke. Elsie gained more than a stepfather—she gained an extended family of skillful weavers: her stepfather's mother, Laura White Wilbell; her stepfather's half-sister, Mow-sha Wilbell Edwards; and Susie Santiago Billy, the wife of Laura Wilbell's son, Cruz Billy. Years later, the tradition was carried on when Susan Billy, granddaughter of Cruz Billy, became a student of Elsie's.

Annie Burke demonstrates the use of the mortar hopper basket, c.1940

Annie Ramon Burke

(1876-1962)

Annie Tomasia Ramon was the daughter of Mary Arnold and Charley Ramon of Cloverdale. Her first husband was George Gomachu of Yorkville, Elsie Allen's father, who died around 1907. Not long after, Annie married Richard Burke of Hopland. Taught from childhood by her mother, Mary Arnold, and grandmother Gunsissie, Annie Burke gained considerable renown for her weaving skills over the course of her life.

During the 1940s, Annie Burke and others formed the Pomo Mothers' Club, later known as the Pomo Indian Women's Club. This Mendocino County organization promoted the social, physical, and financial health of Pomo people through education, social networking, and fundraising. Basketry exhibits and demonstrations proved to be an effective medium for educating non-Indians about Pomo traditions. However, when requests began to pour in from San Francisco museums and North Coast service organizations, the weavers had few baskets to show: most weavers honored the tribal tradition of burying baskets with their makers, and many sold their pieces or gave them to relatives and friends. The club resorted to borrowing baskets from white collectors (such as the John and Grace Hudson collection then owned by nephew Mark Carpenter) to supplement their limited supply.

Annie Burke, a woman of strong character, decided to defy the tradition of burying all of a woman's baskets with her. She began assembling her own collection, with the help of her daughter, Elsie Allen, who later wrote, "Mother told me that she did not want this to happen with her as she wanted me to have her baskets to help me when I started up basketweaving again."[2]

Upon Annie Burke's death in 1962, the torch passed from mother to daughter. Elsie Allen continued to use the collection to educate people, supplementing it over the years not only with the work of others, but with many of her own pieces.

Annie Burke, cooking basket, n.d. (EA #129)

"This basket is in pristine condition. Annie Burke must have made it strictly for show. It's very simple, yet beautiful."—Susan Billy[3]

Annie and Richard Burke, c.1910.

"My father died when I was about eight and my mother soon after that married Mr. Richard Burke... he was a very kind stepfather to me."

—Elsie Allen[4]

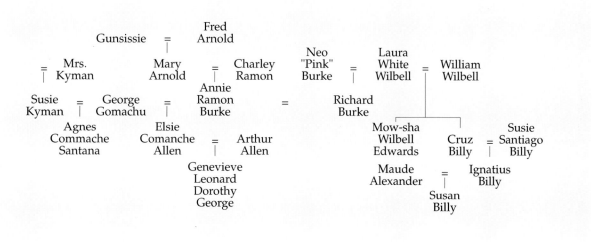

This selective genealogy illustrates the relationships among the weavers in Elsie Allen's immediate family. It does not include all family members.

This handpainted photograph shows four generations of basketweavers: (L–R) Gunsissie (Fannie) Arnold, Mary Arnold, Annie Ramon Burke, and the infant Elsie Comanche, c.1900

"I'm the fourth generation of basketweavers: my great-grandmother, my grandmother, my mother... That's how I learned."—Elsie Allen[5]

Mary Arnold
(1845–1925)

Mary Arnold was the only daughter of Englishman Fred (Brad) Arnold and Gunsissie. With Charley Ramon ("Lamon"), Mary Arnold had two children: Annie Tomasia Ramon (Burke) and a boy, Visenthe Ramon. Mary Arnold later married Lee Lilly of Lake County and, after his death in 1905, Willie Williams of Pinoleville.

Elsie Allen lived with her maternal grandmother, Mary Arnold, near Cloverdale until she was about eight years old. For the next three years she lived near Hopland with a more extended family that included her mother and stepfather (Annie and Richard Burke), Mary Arnold, and Gunsissie. Elsie Allen remembered working with her mother and grandmother as a child and into her early twenties, gathering materials and making baskets: "My grandmother weaved one-willow and three-willow basket. She weaved great big ones. She never weaved small ones."[6]

"Not only did I lose her help," Elsie Allen reflected about her grandmother's death, "but most of her examples of baskets as well, as it was customary for an Indian woman to have all her baskets and reeds buried with her."[7] Mary Arnold is identified as the weaver of one basket in the Elsie Allen Collection, a beaded "goblet" made in 1916.

Mary Arnold, gift basket, 1916
(EA #64)

Elsie Allen's student Marion Steinbach noted that Elsie's grandmother Mary Arnold based the form of this basket on a kerosene lamp.[8]

Agnes Santana, c.1930s

"I got acquainted with her when I stayed in Cloverdale. Together we would go fishing and sit along the river. Me and Agnes. We used to catch four, five, or six. We lucky enough, maybe eight."—Laura Somersal[9]

Agnes Commache Santana
(1877–1974)

Agnes Commache[10] Santana was the daughter of George Gomachu (Comanche) of Yorkville and his first wife, Susie Kyman of Cloverdale. Born in Cloverdale, Agnes lived much of her life there with her husband, Maslino Santana, their son, John, and a daughter, Lillian, from Agnes' marriage to Fred Jack. In 1918, the Santanas lost an infant son, Robert, to the flu epidemic.

Throughout her life, Mrs. Santana maintained a strong relationship with her half-sister, Elsie Allen. According to John Santana, there were frequent visits between his family in Cloverdale and Elsie's in Pinoleville. Agnes also became close to Dry Creek weaver Laura Somersal, a distant relative through Laura's marriage to Jim Somersal, who was the half-brother of Agnes' first husband, Fred Jack. In about 1929, Laura moved with her husband to Cloverdale, where he had property. John Santana remembers Laura and Agnes visiting often and weaving together: "They knew each other pretty well... [If] Laura needed some roots, they would trade. [Agnes would] go over there and Laura would come over here and they'd weave and visit, that's about the way it was."[11]

John Santana describes his mother's weaving: "Most of them were just the regular root baskets... She didn't make the baskets to sell, but that was one way of making a little money when they needed it... She enjoyed making the baskets, that was more or less a hobby for her... Whenever she'd have a grandchild, she'd make them a basket, sometimes two."[12]

Agnes Santana wove baskets until she was well into her eighties, slowed only by failing eyesight and arthritis.

Agnes Santana's Grandmother (Mrs. Kyman)

Little is known about the grandmother of Elsie's half-sister, except that she was a Southern Pomo weaver. In her 1928 Indian enrollment application, Agnes Santana stated her mother's family name was Kyman. Laura Somersal remembered Agnes' grandmother as Mrs. Gymana. The hopper basket in the Allen Collection (EA #33) woven by Agnes Santana's grandmother was a gift to Mrs. Allen from Agnes.

Agnes Santana, coiled basket, n.d. (EA #136)

"She enjoyed making the baskets, that was more or less a hobby for her...
Whenever she'd have a grandchild, she'd make them a basket, sometimes
two."—John Santana[13]

Mrs. Kyman, mortar hopper, late 19th century (EA #33)
Elsie's half-sister, Agnes Santana, gave her grandmother's basket to Elsie as a gift.

"A number of bands of lattice twine are added for strength where the basket
will be cut off. The basket ends are trimmed at cut edge to make the hopper.
The original bottom is used again as a starter for another hopper with new
warp sticks added." —Elsie Allen[14]

Laura Wilbell, burden basket, c.1901

Laura Wilbell made this basket for her daughter-in-law Annie Burke to take baby
Vivian "Bibb" Burke's diapers to the river for washing. Note this basket in the family
photograph taken in the hop fields, p.14.

Laura White Wilbell
(1855–1942)

Laura White Wilbell was born on the Mendocino Coast at Noyo, near Fort Bragg. Her mother was Mariana of Yorkville, and her father was a non-Indian named Bob White. Laura married Neo ("Pink") Burke with whom she had Richard Burke, Elsie Allen's stepfather. She later married William Wilbell, a Lake County Indian, whose moniker "Billy" became the family name. Her son by this marriage, Cruz Billy, was the grandfather of Susan Billy. The Wilbells had two daughters, Mow-sha (Manuella) and Catherine (possibly also known as Laura). Mrs. Wilbell raised two granddaughters when her own daughters died while still young: Marion Edwards (Wilder) and Florenda Arnold (Hansen).

Laura Wilbell is seated second from the left surrounded by her family at the Hewlitt Ranch, Hopland, c.1905. Standing (L–R): Laura Wilbell's son Cruz Billy, daughter Laura Billy, son Dick Burke, daughter-in-law Susie Billy, son-in-law Louis Arnold, daughter Mow-sha. Seated (L–R): husband William Wilbell, Laura herself, Cecilia Joaquin and baby, granddaughter Mabel Billy, and two unidentified people.

Mow-sha and her husband, Charlie Edwards Jr., c.1908

Mow-sha Wilbell Edwards

(1892–1909)

Mow-sha, whose name is listed in a 1928 Indian enrollment record as Manuella Billy, was one of Laura and William Wilbell's children. She married Charlie Edwards Jr., son of Tudy Marie Arnold and Charlie Edwards Sr. from Echo, a hamlet in the Russian River Canyon at the northern end of Sonoma County.

Mow-sha and Charlie Edwards' only child was Marion Edwards (Wilder), born in 1909 at the Hewlitt Ranch near Hopland. Mow-sha died a month after giving birth, and Marion grew up with her maternal grandmother, Laura Wilbell.

Charlie Edwards Jr. had a half-sister, Susie Santiago, who married Mow-sha's brother Cruz Billy, creating a dual link between the two families.

Mow-sha Wilbell Edwards, storage basket, 1908 (EA #38)

This basket belonged to Mow-sha's half-brother Richard Burke. It later became known in the family as "Tha Tha's [Grandpa's] sox basket." Elsie Allen repaired the rim.

Left: Susie Billy and Cruz Billy with baby daughter Mabel, 1901

Below: The Billy family on the occasion of Susie and Cruz Billy's fiftieth wedding anniversary. Standing (L–R): Matthew Billy, Katherine Billy Yepez, Dennis Billy, and Ignatius Billy, Hopland, c.1950. Leonard Yepez, photographer

Susie Santiago Billy

(1885-1968)

Susie Santiago Billy was born in 1885 to Silva Santiago and Tudy Marie Arnold. Susie Billy's father was likely one of the Sandiego family of the Kashaya Pomo. About 1900, Susie married Cruz Billy, a leader at the Hopland Rancheria. Cruz Billy and Richard Burke (Elsie Allen's stepfather) were half-brothers, making Mrs. Susie Billy Elsie Allen's aunt.

The Billys had twelve children, one of whom, Ignatius, fathered weaver and guest curator Susan Billy. It was Ignatius' collection of his mother's baskets that inspired the younger Susan Billy to learn the art of Pomo basketry: "I remember visiting my grandma when I was five. I remember her sitting outside her back door in the driveway under the walnut tree working on a basket. I was told my grandma was always working on a basket."[15]

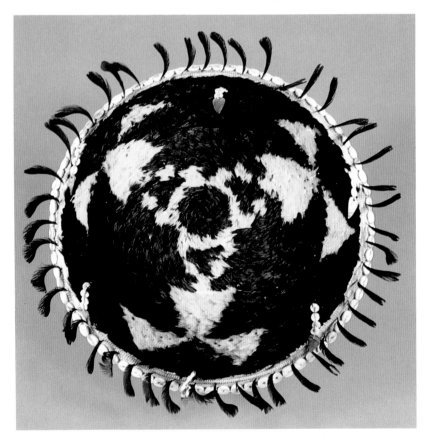

Susie Santiago Billy, gift basket, n.d. (EA #130)

Even though Elsie Allen taught Susan Billy to weave, Susan's grandmother Susie Billy was, in a sense, the young weaver's teacher too. Elsie explains: "My mother... never weaved feather baskets. I learned from my great-aunt Mrs. Susie Billy."[16]

Susan Billy demonstrates coiling, Hopland, 1985. Ralph T. "Ted" Coe, photographer.

This photograph appeared in the exhibition and catalog developed by Ted Coe, *Lost and Found Traditions: Native American Art, 1965–1985,* in which Susan was a featured artist.

Susan Billy
(1951–)

Susan Billy was born in Hot Springs, South Dakota, but her tribal ancestry connects her to the Hopland Rancheria in Mendocino County, California. Susan's father, Ignatius L. Billy, left Hopland after graduating from high school and doing ranch work with his father, Cruz, for two years. He attended Riverside Junior College, receiving an Associate of Arts degree in 1938, and then transferred to the University of California at Berkeley, where he graduated with a Bachelor of Arts in 1940. It was while living at UC Berkeley's International House that Ignatius met his future bride, Maude Alexander.

Susan is the youngest of their four children. Her oldest brother, Glen, and his two sons live in the Bay Area; her sister, Madeline, raises her family in Switzerland; and her brother David lives with his wife and two sons in New Mexico. Susan lives with her daughter, Dawn, in Ukiah.

"I remember ice skating every day in the winter, and swimming all summer long—it was a happy time for me," Susan recalls of her childhood in the Dakotas. In 1958, Mr. Billy was transferred to Washington, D.C., where he would spend the rest of his career. When the family settled in Arlington, Virginia, Susan was in the second grade. It was during these early years that her fascination with Pomo baskets began. Her father had several baskets that his mother, Susie Billy, had made. Susan recalls the great reverence that surrounded the baskets:

> I knew they were not toys! My mind began to wander and open towards these baskets—I wanted to know more. Being raised far from my tribe, my people, my relatives, I had only my father to rely on. So I would ask him about the materials, the designs, and how did my grandmother make them? Many times my father told me that someday I could come and ask my aunt Elsie—and she could answer all my questions! I don't think anyone ever thought I really would!

After attending college at Virginia Commonwealth University in Richmond, Susan left home to travel, heading first to southern California and then to Hawaii before moving to Seattle. Feeling "rained out," she went to Mexico and lived on the beach for three months, until, "The baskets began to call me—living in another culture reminded me I had a purpose, a need, a desire—I wanted to know about the baskets."

Settling first in the Bay Area, then moving onto the Hopland Rancheria in November 1973, Susan now set a steady course. Knocking on Elsie Allen's door at Pinoleville in February of 1974, she began her apprenticeship. They worked together five and sometimes six days a week. Some days they drove to see how the plants were

Susan Billy, miniature gift basket, c.1975 (EA #122)

"After Elsie had taken me to the [Mendocino] County Museum to show me her 'mini-on-the-head-of-a-pin,' I wanted to make a small basket... I made it in an afternoon and just gave it to her. This was my first miniature basket."
—Susan Billy[17]

growing. Some days were gathering days. Sometimes it was Elsie's teaching day, and they would drive north to Covelo or Willits to give a class on basketweaving. Other days she would be demonstrating somewhere. Elsie made it clear that she had much to teach and give—and there was no time to waste.

In June of 1977, D-Q University (Davis, California) awarded Susan an Associate of Arts Degree in Native American Studies, through its Independent Study Program, for her work with Elsie. In 1978 and 1979 Elsie and Susan were invited to participate for one year in the California Arts Council's Master–Apprentice Program, funded by the National Endowment for the Arts.

Susan travelled in 1977 to Kansas City, Missouri, to the Nelson Gallery–Atkins Museum to demonstrate Pomo basketry at the exhibit *Sacred Circles: Two Thousand Years of North American Indian Art.* This occasion represented her first time demonstrating on her own, without Elsie. She and Elsie were scheduled to go together, but important family concerns kept Elsie home. Lake County Pomo weaver and healer Mabel McKay also demonstrated her weaving skills at the *Sacred Circles* exhibit.

Susan joined Elsie on a 1983 trip to New York City, when Elsie consulted with the American Museum of Natural History and the Museum of the American Indian (Heye Foundation) about the museums' Pomo collections. While in New York, the pair demonstrated at Hunter College and a Native American art gallery. In the same year, Susan started Bead Fever. Originally operated out of her home, today Bead Fever is a successful storefront business in downtown Ukiah.

Over the years, weaver and teacher Susan Billy has participated in numerous cultural programs, including Festival at the Lake in Oakland and the Traditional Indian Skills Program at Kule Loklo, Point Reyes National Seashore. Her involvement in museum exhibitions is extensive and includes: *Lost and Found Traditions: Native American Art, 1965–1985* at the American Museum of Natural History (1985); *Dialogue with Tradition,* a contemporary exhibit developed in 1991 by the Brooklyn Museum to accompany its *Objects of Myth and Memory* (both exhibits travelled to the Oakland Museum in 1992); and the *Art of the Americas* wing at San Francisco's deYoung Museum (1992). Susan served as a guest curator for a premiere exhibition at the Smithsonian's National Museum of the American Indian (George Gustav Heye Center) in New York City in 1994. As a relative and student of Elsie Allen's, she co-curated *Remember Your Relations: The Elsie Allen Baskets, Family & Friends.*

Basketmaking tools—a knife, an awl, and two basketry starts

"... and when I walked into her classroom,... she had a basket-making awl and a knife in her hand, and she just held them out to me, and she said, 'Here. These are yours.' And I looked at them, and I could tell they were old, and she just looked, looked me right in the eye, and she said, 'These had belonged to your grandmother [Susie Billy], and when your grandmother passed away, they were given to me... I realized that I'd only been holding them for you'... When I held them, I just felt really full. I also felt totally blessed to have them."—Susan Billy[18]

Rhoda Knight, coiled basket, c.1930s (EA #51)

Rhoda Knight's three-rod (stick) coiled baskets are outstanding examples of a very challenging technique. Mrs. Knight preferred black root (bulrush) for her designs and never did use redbud, according to her daughter Virginia Knight Buck.[1]

Extended Family

◆◆◆◆◆◆◆◆◆◆◆◆◆◆◆◆◆◆◆◆◆◆◆◆◆◆

Marriage relationships forged connections between Elsie Allen and weavers Rhoda Somersal Knight, Ethel Knight Burke, and Gladys Myers Lockhart. Rhoda Knight and Gladys Lockhart were related to Elsie through her husband, Arthur Allen. Ethel Burke married Elsie's stepbrother, "Bibb," making Ethel and Elsie sisters-in-law. These three women were born within ten years of Elsie, sharing family connections as well as the experiences of the times in which they grew up.

Arthur Allen, 1942. Michael Harrison, photographer

Rhoda Somersal Knight
(1890-1958)

Rhoda Somersal Knight was born at Manchester on the Mendocino coast to Nellie White and Jack Somersal. Her mother, also a weaver, moved with Rhoda to Yokayo Rancheria when her daughter married the Pomo community leader and activist Stephen Knight. The Knights had three children. The Somersal and Knight families have several links to Elsie Allen's family, and Rhoda Knight's daughter Virginia (now Virginia Buck) added to the connection when she married Lawrence Allen, Elsie's brother-in-law.

Rhoda was an expert weaver of three-stick baskets, with the skill and stamina to produce a difficult traditional design. According to Virginia Knight Buck her mother's baskets were made with "a pattern that's been carried on from a long time ago. She's the only one [who continued to] use it... I think it's too much work so the others didn't do it."[2]

Rhoda Knight, Yokayo Rancheria, c.1946. Michael Harrison, photographer

In 1981, Elsie Allen reflected with characteristic understatement on Rhoda Knight's skill: "She was known as a pretty good basketweaver. Her baskets always [were] nice... Even willow, even root, and fine."[3]

Ethel Knight Burke
(1906–1995)

Ethel Knight Burke, the daughter of Emma Somersal and Jimmy Knight, was born near the Yokayo Rancheria. She learned to weave from her maternal grandmother, Nellie White. Her aunt on her father's side was the highly-regarded Pomo weaver Mary Knight Benson. In 1923, Ethel married Vivian "Bibb" Burke, Elsie Allen's stepbrother, and they settled in the Hopland house where Elsie had spent much of her youth. Although they had no children of their own, the Burkes raised several sons and daughters of family members.

Mrs. Burke recalled her mother weaving, but that her basketmaking was limited by the needs of her thirteen children. Ethel spent much of her childhood on the Yokayo Rancheria with her maternal aunt, weaver Rhoda Knight. It was Rhoda who showed her how to weave a three-rod (or "three-stick") basket.

While in her early twenties, Ethel began weaving actively. She preferred weaving the one-stick technique her grandmother had taught her to the three-stick technique, explaining that "it's quick, you get through with it. I want to see how it looks."[4]

Left: Ethel Burke, Hopland Rancheria, c.1930s

"When I moved to the Hopland Rancheria, I didn't know anyone at all in the valley. Auntie Ethel and her husband, Bibb, always made me feel welcome in their home; we'd sit by the fire and drink tea, and laugh and talk. It felt like family to me."
—Susan Billy[5]

Right: Ethel Burke, coiled basket, n.d. (EA #135)

"That is a beautiful rim. It's so tight and so perfect. Nothing wrong with that rim. It's very smooth."
—Ethel Knight Burke[6]

Gladys Lockhart as a young woman, c.1915

"My mother was a very gracious, dignified lady... such a strong woman [and] very gifted."—Lois Lockart Compton[7]

Gladys Myers Lockhart
(1899–1972)

Gladys Myers was born in 1899 to Joe Myers and Nellie McGee, and grew up on the Pinoleville Rancheria, just north of the Ukiah city limit. As a young woman, she married and had a family with John Knight (brother of Ethel Knight Burke) of Hopland. Later she married Lou Lockhart of the Sherwood Valley Rancheria near Willits. She was a first cousin of Elsie Allen's husband, Arthur Allen. It was the marriage of Elsie and Arthur Allen that led to the representation of Gladys Lockhart's miniatures in the Allen Collection: the baskets were made as a birthday gift to her cousin Arthur.

Gladys Lockhart wove a variety of baskets, including feather baskets, three-stick baskets, and miniatures. Her daughter Lois Lockart Compton recalls:

> [I'd] sit there and watch, and I'd think, "Mama, how can you weave that basket and not make a mistake?" She never missed a stitch. She'd sit there and she'd be going along weaving... putting the root in there between the sticks, push[ing] it through, all really fast, and I noticed that she was doing a pattern. And I said, "How did you do that?" I was looking around for a piece of paper that had the pattern on it, and then it dawned on me, she has that in her head. I asked, "How do you know how far to go with the design?" She said, "I just know, it's just in our people. Some of our people are gifted."[8]

Remembering her mother, Lois Lockart Compton took these words of hers to heart: "Know who you are and be proud of what you are and who you are—but don't ever think you're better than anyone else."[9]

Gladys Lockhart, miniature gift baskets, n.d. (clockwise from left: EA #121, 119, 120)

"Arthur Allen was my mother's first cousin. They were close friends. She made these little baskets for him... as a birthday gift. She said she did this to see how small she could get them."—Lois Lockart Compton[10]

Annie Lake, gift baskets (clockwise from top: EA #62, 61, 66, 67, 69, 68, 65)

A Cohort of Friends

◆◆◆◆◆◆◆◆◆◆◆◆◆◆◆◆◆◆◆◆◆◆◆◆

Pomo women born at the end of the 19th century typically learned weaving as young girls sitting alongside their mothers or grand-mothers. They came of age during the Arts and Crafts Movement (c.1890s–1920s), a time when collectors began to value handwork by Native Americans. Many baskets were woven for this burgeoning private and museum market, and some weavers were able to make a decent living by their art.

Other basketweavers found that the demands of marriage and family precluded any serious effort to weave. It was only later in life when their children were grown that they could rededicate themselves to the demanding but deeply satisfying pursuit of Pomo basketweaving. This dedication brought women together and created bonds of common interest and friendship that lasted many decades. With a commitment similar to Elsie Allen's, they were generous with their time—teaching, demonstrating, and consulting.

Elsie Allen, born in 1899, was slightly younger than most of the weavers profiled here, all of whom lived very long lives: Annie Burke Lake was the eldest (b. 1887), followed by Laura Fish Somersal (b. 1892), Mollie Wright Jackson (b. 1895), and Alice Conner Elliott (b. 1896). Mollie Jackson and Laura Somersal were special friends of Elsie Allen. In recognition of the connections between teachers and students, two other weavers are included here: Evelyn Lake (b. 1908) and Myrtle McKay Chavez (b. 1939). Evelyn learned weaving from her mother, Annie Lake, and Myrtle from her mother's aunt Laura Somersal.

Annie Lake and Elsie Allen at Mrs. Lake's home, Redwood Valley Rancheria, 1985. Marion Steinbach, photographer

Annie Lake, Redwood Valley Rancheria, 1959. George Ward, photographer

This photograph of Annie Lake on the porch of her home was taken during a visit by Mark Carpenter. Carpenter was the nephew of artist Grace Carpenter Hudson, who devoted years to recording Pomo life through her paintings.

"When I was a little girl, my mother, Lulu, washed for your grandmother, Helen McCowen Carpenter, and Mrs. Carpenter asked me my name, and I told her I did not have one, and she said, 'Your name is Annie,' and she gave me a kerchief and a ribbon for my hair—I am seventy-two years old now, and my name is still Annie."—Annie Lake[1]

Annie Burke Lake

(1887–1988)

Born on the Held-Burke Ranch, Annie Burke was the daughter of Sam Burke (a Yokayo Pomo) and Lulu DeShield (Dashiell), from Round Valley. After the death of their mother, Annie raised her half-sister Stella Fred (Tooley), daughter of Lulu and George Fred. In about 1905 Annie married Harris Lake of Pinoleville, a graduate of the Riverside Indian School (Sherman Institute). Together the Lakes had ten children of whom only two, Evelyn and Vernetta, lived to adulthood. Her husband and both daughters predeceased Mrs. Lake, who lived for more than one hundred years.

Annie Lake worked in the fields, did woodworking, quilting, dressmaking, and basketweaving all of her life. A prolific weaver, she was known particularly for her distinctive coiled gift baskets, both beaded and feathered, a number of which were purchased or otherwise collected by Elsie Allen.

Annie Lake, serving basket, c. 1945
(EA #47)
Elsie Allen used this spectacular basket as a bread platter.

Evelyn Lake

(1908–c.1952)

Evelyn Lake, born at Pinoleville Rancheria, was the older of Annie and
Harris Lake's two surviving daughters. Evelyn married Floyd Potter
with whom she had a son. Her goddaughter Evangeline Duncan
remembers that tiny coiled baskets were Evelyn's specialty. She probably
learned this skill from her mother, who also specialized in coiled work.
Evangeline has childhood memories of joining her godmother and her
aunt Annie on gathering trips in Redwood Valley: "I used to help Annie
and Evelyn. We went down to the [Russian] river together to gather
roots. There were hardly any houses there then..."[2] Evelyn died in
about 1952, still in her forties, decades before her mother.

Evelyn Lake, miniature basket, 1943–44 (EA #87)

Evelyn Lake's goddaughter Evangeline Duncan remembers that
tiny coiled baskets were Evelyn's specialty.[3]

Laura Fish Somersal

(1892–1990)

Laura Fish Somersal was the daughter of Mary John Eli of the Wappo people of Geyserville and Bill Fish, Southern Pomo of Cloverdale. She was born on the John Stone Ranch near Geyserville. Laura worked much of her life at a variety of jobs—as a cook, a hop picker, and housekeeper. She became a Somersal when she married her third husband, Jim Somersal, brother of Yokayo weavers Rhoda Somersal Knight and Emma Somersal Knight. She had one foster son, George, and raised a number of other children as part of her extended family.

Because her mother, Mary Eli, was blind, Laura learned weaving from others. Her cousin Jack Woho, who learned to weave from his mother, gave her her first basket start when she was a young girl. He told her, "Here, you'll be a woman someday, and I'd like to see you work on this."[4] Mrs. Somersal remembered learning to weave from Jack's mother (her aunt) and from a woman friend of her brother's named Rosa Thomas.

Although she learned to weave as a child, Mrs. Somersal became most active as a weaver later in life. The Wappo and Pomo people speak very different languages, but they have been neighbors for centuries and many aspects of their cultures, including basketry, are very similar. As Mrs. Somersal said, "They all do the same weave."[5] She learned a wide range of basketry skills and earned a reputation as a master weaver of Pomo forms.

By 1970, when she was in her late seventies, Laura had become sought-after as a language consultant, teacher, and demonstrator. She

Laura Somersal, miniature baskets. (L–R, Rear: EA #100, 90; Front: EA #106, 104, 102, 105)

"It took me eight hours to make this size. It is harder [than standard size coiling]. It is hard to hold. It pops out of your hand... You don't put sticks [willow foundation rods] in these little tiny ones. You just twist this [sedge] and make it look like a stick.—Laura Somersal[6]

Laura Somersal with her student and niece, Myrtle McKay Chavez, Warm Springs Dam site, Sonoma County, c.1980. Scott M. Patterson, photographer

"The one good thing about Auntie is that she never helped you, she really sat there and told you. At least she did me, and the cleaning of the root I had to do myself. I don't know how many times she made me rip the basket out and go around again. She made sure I learned right. She showed me what my mistake was and told me what to do. Sometimes I'd be in a hurry and I'd put two stitches in one, and she would tell me to take it out. Or, I don't connect the rod right and have to take it out. She was a good teacher."

—Myrtle McKay Chavez[7]

Laura Somersal with sedge root at Dry Creek, Sonoma County, 1979. Scott M. Patterson, photographer

"Elsie and I were good friends... we used to go to Sacramento. They gave us a platform to sit at with our work. We did that together. Whatever we have we were working on we would take. We sell what we could... just ask for so much and then if they can afford it, it's okay. If they can't, you can't just give it away." —Laura Somersal[8]

taught weaving and her native Wappo at Sonoma State University, the University of California at Berkeley, and Ya-ka-ama (an Indian-run educational center and native plant nursery in Sonoma County), among other places. Mrs. Somersal also felt comfortable instructing students at her home on the Dry Creek Rancheria: "They bring their work with them. Two would sit over there and one would sit over there. If it's five, one sits on the bed."[9]

Laura recalls meeting Elsie Allen in 1899 or 1900:

> I was between eight and nine; I wasn't a young lady yet... They had a [Big] Time below the Alexander Valley Bridge. They had a cabin there and they always celebrate like when new things come in—they used to raise corn on the river... [Elsie] was a baby in a basket. That's why I went to her mother... I went over to her and I understood the language. She spoke the same language my father did, so I understood what she said. I guess I couldn't talk it back, I just understood. I stood around there until I picked the baby up and she asked me if I wanted to carry it on my back. I said yeah. I used the Indian word... [Later in life Elsie] took me around to gather redbud and things like that, black roots...[10]

As friends, weavers, and elders, Laura Somersal and Elsie Allen often spent time together, sometimes with Mollie Jackson of Pinoleville. It was Elsie who introduced Laura to the use of pheasant feathers in coiled basketweaving. In 1979, they traveled together to New York City for the opening of *The Ancestors, Native Artists of the Americas* exhibition at the Museum of the American Indian, Heye Foundation.

Myrtle McKay Chavez
(1939–)

A longtime resident of Windsor, Sonoma County, Myrtle McKay Chavez was born on the Big Valley Rancheria near Lakeport. She is the daughter of Pearl Martin (Pomo from Geyserville) and Fred McKay (a Wintun from Hayfork, Trinity County). Myrtle is related to two well-known Pomo basketweavers: Mabel McKay of Lake County, her father's sister; and Laura Somersal of Dry Creek Rancheria, her mother's aunt.

Beginning in 1971 while she was still in her thirties, Myrtle had the good fortune to learn weaving from Laura Somersal. She recalls:

> There was a neighbor of mine who wanted to go to basket classes, which I didn't want to go to. I knew that Auntie started teaching, but I didn't want to go. I didn't think I wanted to learn baskets. Then my neighbor convinced me that it was relaxation, so I went with her. I learned to weave the baskets, and she didn't.[11]

Soon, Myrtle began to enjoy the work and did well. The younger weaver continued to study with Laura over the years, and in 1990 Laura praised, "I'm her teacher, and she's doing good."[12] Myrtle credits Elsie Allen with teaching her how to weave with feathers. She still weaves and takes commissions for her work.

Myrtle McKay Chavez harvesting sedge, Warm Springs Dam site, c.1980. Scott M. Patterson, photographer

Myrtle McKay Chavez, canoe basket, n.d. (EA #57)

This basket became part of the Allen collection when Myrtle "sold it to Genny" [Aguilar].[13]

Mollie Wright Jackson
(1895–1982)

Mollie Wright Jackson, daughter of Kate Anchor and Charley Wright, traced her heritage to the Little River Pomo of the Mendocino coast. Her family acquired the name of Wright through their working relationship with Redwood Valley rancher Berry Wright. About 1912, Mollie Wright married Andrew Jackson, with whom she had ten children. In 1933, the Jackson family left Redwood Valley and settled on the Pinoleville Rancheria, just north of Ukiah. Remarkably, given the size of her family, Mollie Jackson was able to remain an active weaver all her life. Mollie's son Robert Jackson recalls joining his mother on gathering trips as a young boy:

> I was lucky in a way, being the little boy, because I got to travel with a lot of older women when they went to dig roots, get willows. We'd go in a wagon, a buckboard, horse-drawn; go down to the Russian River, up to where the dam [Lake Mendocino] is now. We didn't go far, maybe as far as Yokayo Rancheria, just what you could cover in a day's time with a horse doing what he wanted to do.[14]

The beauty of Mrs. Jackson's work reflects the great care she took in gathering and preparing her weaving materials:

> My mother was a particular woman when it came to gathering

Mollie Jackson, work basket, c.1930 (EA #36)

"I admired the acorn drying baskets she [Mollie Jackson] made for Elsie. That was nice."—Laura Somersal[15]

willows; she just didn't pick anything... It was more quality than quantity to her... [To] get the shoots even [she used] glass to smooth the willows out... or sharp knives... I asked her and she wouldn't tell me how she made it like that, but she used to feel that. I think it was in her touch. It was amazing...[16]

Mollie Jackson maintained close friendships with a number of her fellow weavers. Salome Alcantra remembered Mollie Jackson as an especially capable woman: "She can do a man's job... like chopping the wood, grapevine clipping, and work in the hop field... she had nice baskets, she knew how to make baskets, beautiful baskets."[17]

Mollie Jackson, Laura Somersal, and Elsie Allen sometimes gave one another baskets as gifts. Laura Somersal particularly admired the acorn drying baskets that Mollie made for Elsie's collection.

Below: Mollie Jackson and Elsie Allen, Pinoleville Rancheria, 1967. Marion Steinbach, photographer

"Mollie Jackson, my friend, yes, she's a nice weaver. She was a good friend of Elsie, too." —Laura Somersal[18]

Right: Mollie Jackson twining a basket outside her home at Pinoleville Rancheria, c.1940

**"She would make baskets mostly in the morning; unless it was raining, she would sit out in the sun."
—Robert Jackson[19]**

Alice Conner Elliott
(1896–1984)

Daughter of Frances and William Conner, Alice Conner Elliott was a lifelong Hopland resident. After the death of her parents when she was a young girl, Alice went to live with her maternal grandparents, Jim and Louise (surname unknown). Alice Elliott first married Peter Jack, and later wed Rayfield Elliott. Several of her children became active as cultural teachers and demonstrators, including the late Mitchell Jack of Hopland, a well-known traditional Pomo singer.

Alice began to weave at the age of nine under her grandmother Louise's tutelage. She became adept at all kinds of baskets—baby baskets, feather baskets, one-stick and three-stick coiled baskets, and twined baskets that she called summer baskets because of the season in which she wove them.

Mrs. Elliott taught her daughter-in-law Bonnie Elliott the art of the baby (or cradle) basket and then encouraged her to teach others. Today Bonnie shares the skills she learned from Alice with a new generation of weavers.

Susan Billy was Mrs. Elliott's next-door neighbor on the Hopland Rancheria in the mid-1970s. Susan approached the elder weaver at that

Alice Elliott, coiled baskets, n.d. (left: EA #53, right: EA #56)

"She told me, 'We go by the rules when we make a basket.' Every design she made represented something she knew [from tradition]…" —Bonnie Elliott[20]

Alice Elliott at home, Hopland Rancheria, 1978. Maude Alexander Billy, photographer

time to ask her to make a basket for the personal collection of her father, Ignatius Billy:

> He was very specific [about] who he wanted a basket [from]: Mollie Jackson, Mabel McKay, Annie Lake, Elsie Allen, Alice Elliott, and Salome [Alcantra]. So I went to each of the women... and asked each of them to make a basket for my father... Not very long [thereafter] Alice, who I lived next door to because I was living on the Hopland Rancheria, called to me... and said she wanted to talk to me... She said, "You know you asked me to make a basket and then you never came back... It's been finished already for two months."... So she finished this basket. By the time my father passed away, she was the only one that made him a basket.[21]

Lake County Weavers

◆◆◆◆◆◆◆◆◆◆◆◆◆◆◆◆◆◆◆◆◆◆◆◆◆

Suzanne Moore Holder, Lydia Anderson Faught, and Annie Dick Boone had much in common. Contemporaries of Elsie Allen, they all lived at Upper Lake Rancheria (northwest of Clear Lake), were related through marriage, and possessed a talent for weaving.

Lydia Faught and Suzanne Holder were sisters-in-law, and both women were related to Annie Boone through Ralph Holder and Lydia Faught's mother, Emma John Gilbert, who was Annie Boone's cousin.

All three of these Lake County weavers excelled at creating baskets rich with colorful designs in bird feathers, and sometimes, when feathers were unavailable, tiny glass beads. It is probable that Elsie collected the work of these women as examples of the distinctive basketry tradition associated with Upper Lake Rancheria.

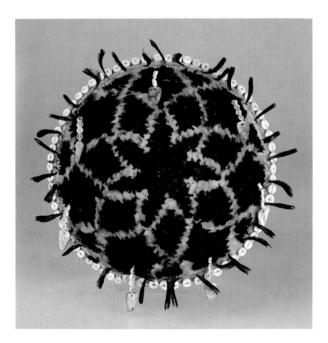

Suzanne Holder, gift basket, n.d. (EA #74)

"Mother used to pinch off [feathers] to work and she would twirl them at the base so they splayed out... they'll be sticking out uneven, so you clip them off and make them even... [After they were] stuck in, my mother would tie it [the basket] up with a rag or handkerchief after she was done, [and] leave it for about two to three days. Then the feathers would lie down flat."—Delvin Holder[1]

Suzanne Holder, gift basket, n.d. (EA #77)

"They buy bird feathers from hunters... My father worked for a man who used to go hunting... He would give the mallard's head to my father and she [Suzanne Holder] would use those."—Delvin Holder[2]

Suzanne Moore Holder
(1899-1982)

Born at Upper Lake, Suzanne Moore Holder was the daughter of Fannie Gilbert and Frank Moore. Her mother died while she was still young, and she was raised by her grandmother Minnie Gilbert. In the late 1920s she married Ralph Holder, also of Upper Lake Rancheria.

Suzanne Holder probably learned weaving from her grandmother. According to her son Delvin Holder, the only types of baskets she wove were feathered, beaded, and baby baskets. Feathered baskets were her specialty: she used meadowlark, bluebird, red-winged blackbird, oriole, woodpecker, and mallard head feathers, and quail topknots. "I know my mother sold to Elsie... She sold her some of the beaded baskets... But she [Suzanne] preferred the feathered. When the feathers weren't available, she would go to the beads."[3]

Suzanne Holder, c.1970.

"My mother... finished one [basket] at a time. If she needed extra money, she would go to Elsie's [to sell her baskets]."
—Delvin Holder[4]

Lydia Faught, gift basket, 1920–25 (EA #63)

"My aunt was the bold one [of the three Upper Lake weavers]. She'd make the designs and it was a design that nobody else would think of... There used to be a frog on the ranch and he used to make noise, you know how they croak. And she would say, 'He's giving me a design.'" —Delvin Holder[5]

Lydia Anderson Faught
(1887–c.1967)

Lydia Anderson Faught (sometimes recorded as "Ford" or "Fort") was born to Emma Bateman and Ed Anderson at Upper Lake. She was the half-sister of renowned beadmaker Ralph Holder, the husband of fellow Upper Lake weaver Suzanne Holder. She married Walter Faught, who died as a young man in the flu epidemic of 1918. Mrs. Faught had two sons, Luther and Fred.

It is likely that Lydia Faught learned to weave from both her mother and her grandmother Alice Woris. The work of her grandmother is found in a number of museum collections. According to her nephew Delvin Holder, Mrs. Faught was an artist skilled in all types of basketmaking, with a special talent for design. Her artistry and business acumen led to a client list including collectors from as far away as Los Angeles and San Diego, enabling her to support herself and her sons.

Lydia Faught, 1951. Mildred E. Van Every, photographer

"She [Lydia Faught] did everything. Anything was her specialty... from way back she had [a] reputation. People know her from places like L.A., San Diego, and distant places."—Delvin Holder[6]

Annie Boone, Upper Lake Rancheria, 1947. Michael Harrison, photographer

Annie Dick Boone

(1889–c.1960)

Annie Dick, born at Upper Lake, was the daughter of Willom (or Willum) Dick and Laura (Laury) Burris, whose family came from Big Valley. She came from an especially gifted family of weavers, including her mother, her paternal grandmother, Sally, and her aunt Rosa Smith. About 1910 Annie Dick married Yonte Boone, and they had no children.

Delvin Holder recalls his mother, Suzanne Holder, saying that of the three Lake County weavers represented in the Allen collection, Annie Boone's work was the finest. According to anthropologist Sally McLendon, Mrs. Boone stands out as a brilliant weaver whose pieces are in a number of museum collections across the country. Some of these collections include fine work she did as a teenager.

Annie Boone, gift basket, n.d. (EA #76)

The 233 feathers on this basket have been cut to a 1/4-inch length after being sewn into the surface, creating distinct areas of color.[7]

Mabel McKay holding sedge, Warm Springs Dam site, Sonoma County, 1980.
Scott M. Patterson, photographer

"I said, 'Mabel, what do you mean the spirit told you [how to weave]? You
mean you didn't watch your grandmother?' She [Mabel McKay] says, 'No, the
spirit moved in my hands. It taught me how. It taught me what to do.' Her
direction was always from the Creator."—Greg Sarris[1]

Healers

◆◆◆◆◆◆◆◆◆◆◆◆◆◆◆◆◆◆◆◆◆◆◆◆

Basketweaving is an all-encompassing art. It requires a deep understanding of the natural world, and of the traditional techniques of harvesting, curing, and preparing the chosen materials. Many of the weaves used by Pomo people require years of apprenticeship and practice to master. Design motifs are passed along through families, or they are discovered in other ways—sometimes through dreams. Each basket can be "read" as a unique process, created by the skilled hands and mind of an individual weaver.

There are cultural rules to be observed throughout the process of making a basket, from husbanding and gathering plant materials to completing the basket itself. Each rule defines how respect must be paid, humility observed, and the personal life of the weaver kept in balance; each stage of the creation of a basket has a spiritual aspect. The late Milton "Bun" Lucas, Kashaya Pomo elder, cultural interpreter, and artist, explains:

> We don't just all gather together and go. We kind of talk about it… [but not] too loud… because it's very sacred to us. They said those roots could hear. The plants could hear, and the road will be rough if we don't just sing a song and go… We have to pray about it… So we have to be very careful where we pick these, and when we pick them, and how to take care of these things.[2]

Elsie Allen talked about some of the spiritual aspects of basketweaving in her book:

> Some old religious beliefs of the Pomo people we carried into the new religion of the Catholic church, and one of those was fasting. We fasted for many things, for example we would fast before starting work on a basket such as a red feather or woodpecker feather basket and would work at it as long as possible and then when we were too hungry we would eat but no longer work on the basket. The fasting was for purification so as to receive help from the Great Spirit in whatever we did.[3]

Weavers, past and present, observe the spiritual side of the weaving tradition; however, only a few weavers

"Ma-yu" (Nora) #226, oil sketch by Grace Carpenter Hudson, 1903. Nora Cooper served as a model for two other works by Ukiah artist Grace Hudson, "A Dancer" #143 (1899) and "Nora" #239 (1904).

are chosen to use their personal powers in the healing of others. The baskets of these medicine women also carry their power. Healing is a spiritual calling, not a personal choice. In an often protracted and gruelling process involving repeated dreaming and emotional trials that lead to self-discovery, the person called—whether man or woman—gradually comes to terms with a new vision of his or her identity and responsibility to others. Healers are not always widely acknowledged for their power; some may practice only within a small social circle, while others are recognized well beyond their immediate communities. The influence of Christianity in native belief systems further affects the perception of traditional healers, creating a range of opinions on the legitimacy and effectiveness of healing practices.

The Elsie Allen Collection includes baskets by three such healers: a still-elusive woman known as Wala-Wala (c.1862–?), Nora Porter Cooper (1887–c.1967), and Salome Bartlett Alcantra (1909–1991). Although we have no evidence that she was a healer, Mrs. Alcantra's mother, Maude Donohue Scott (1884–1945), appears in this section out of respect for the family ties that link so many of the weavers in the Allen collection.

Several accounts exist of how Nora Cooper and Salome Alcantra came to their professions as healers. For Mrs. Cooper, the sources are notes by Dr. John W. Hudson and a 1993 interview with her grandson Keith Pike of Guidiville.[4] For Mrs. Alcantra, the source is a 1990 interview with Dot Brovarney.[5]

One well-known healer and weaver of Mrs. Allen's generation not represented in the collection is Mabel McKay (1907–1993), aunt of weaver Myrtle McKay Chavez. A Lake County resident much of her life, with strong ties to Kashaya spiritual leader Essie Parrish, Mrs. McKay found an integral expression of her own spiritual power in basketweaving. During her long life, Mabel McKay worked with many scholars and students of Pomo culture, sharing her knowledge with wide general audiences.

In 1994, Greg Sarris, now a professor of English at UCLA and former tribal chair of the Coast Miwok, published *Mabel McKay: Weaving the Dream,* a personal account of his longtime friendship with his mentor. In this book he describes the inseparable nature of her weaving and her healing:

> The spirit talked to her constantly now. A voice sounded inside of her and all around her at the same time… "Am I going crazy?" she asked once, hearing the voice in the room and feeling her tongue move in her throat. "No, it's me. And what is happening is that you have an extra tongue. Your throat has been fixed for singing and sucking out the diseases I've been teaching you about. It's talking. It's me in you." "Well, how am I to suck?" Mabel asked. "You'll know when you get to that point. You will have a basket to spit out the disease. All your baskets will come from me. Like I told you."[6]

Elsie Allen herself observed some traditional spiritual practices in her weaving and in what she taught others, but she was not a healer. According to her friend and fellow weaver Laura Somersal, Mrs. Allen did make a pheasant feather basket for Mrs. Somersal's niece Genevieve Marrufo to use in her healing.

This family photograph taken c.1917 shows weaver Maude Scott (standing far right) with her family. Rear (L–R): young Salome Bartlett; her half-brother Elmer Marando; his wife, Lena Wright Marando (weaver Mollie Jackson's sister); Maude herself. Front (L–R): Salome's grandparents Sally and Jack Donohue; Salome's brother, Hastings Bartlett.

Nora Porter Cooper
(1887–c.1967)

Daughter of Sam and Clara Porter, Nora Porter Cooper was born in the Ukiah Valley. A note in artist Grace Hudson's handwriting on the back of a studio photograph of Nora Porter as a teenager [see page 82] indicates that she was sent to the Riverside School, also known as Sherman Institute, a federal Indian school in Riverside, California. There she would have been taught the largely vocational curriculum deemed appropriate for Indian children under federal policy, and there she would have met and lived with other young Indian people from all over California.

Some time after returning to the Ukiah area, Nora Porter married John Cooper, who was born Cooper Beefe. The couple settled at Guidiville, then called Mushtown, on the eastern side of the Ukiah Valley. The Coopers' children included Minerva, Vivian, Tony, and Thomas. Grandson Keith Pike (son of Minerva) remembers Nora Cooper owning and running a horse ranch, growing grapes, and making baskets, executing patterns that "came out of her head."

> She was an artist, a basketweaver... during the day she would make her baskets when it got too warm to work outside. She had these huge collections of baskets. She had little ones and huge conical things... I remember as a kid it was normal to have all these willows and water things and dowels laying around, and half the time she gave them away. Then other times she sold them when she needed money... It was like a living workshop.[7]

Nora Cooper, coiled basket, n.d. (EA #55)

There is a single basket in the Allen collection by Nora Cooper, very similar to the baskets that Mrs. Cooper made for all her children and grandchildren:

"Each of the baskets was blessed in a ceremony and given to us... The design is the same on each of them, the pattern and shape and size. I have one just like that, I've had it for 34 years... It's identical, it's the same thing."—Keith Pike[8]

Weaver Nora Porter (Cooper) with Rosa
Bartlett (right) c.1900. Prob. A.O.
Carpenter, photographer

At some point in her adult life, Nora Porter received a dream and became
a healer. A two-page manuscript in the Hudson Museum collection
purports to tell her story, and although there are inconsistencies between
the Hudson story and the family history as told by her grandson, portions
of the account are worth quoting here for their insight into the process of
becoming a healer, or *Ma-tu.*

> She was growing to be a big girl. Her grandfather, Tony of Potter
> Valley, was a Ma-tu, and as far back as they knew the ancestors had
> had a Ma-tu in the family… always seeing things and she was
> determined not to be a Ma-tu… When fishing again, she saw a Pcu
> ma-ca (fish woman) sitting on a rock, about eight feet above the
> ground.

> The Pcu ma-ca was like a woman to the navel and below like a
> great fish with scales as large as saucers. And she had a great cape
> of scales. The Pcu ma-ca told Ka-ko pi-tum [Nora] she was to be a
> doctor and placed her heavy cape of scales around her shoulders
> and sang two songs to her that she was to learn and sing…

> Ka-ko pi-tum fell unconscious. Another girl dragged her to the
> camp where the grandfather Ma-tu attended her. He said, "My
> daughter, it is no use to rebel. The spirits want you to be a doctor. I
> did not want to be a doctor and refused for eight years, while I was
> working in the mill in Sonoma County… I got sick and had to do it.
> If you refuse the spirits, you will be a sick woman all your life. You
> will have headaches, sick stomach and many evils."

> Still Ka-ko pi-tum was determined not to be a doctor. Her health
> began to decline… Then she tried visiting the sick as a friendly call,
> and incidentally laying her hands on them. At night she would have
> all of their symptoms and the next day they would be much better.

> The Pcu ma-ca came to her more times and taught her two more
> songs… And voices began talking to her… They bade her and are still
> bidding her to heal the insane at the big State Hospital nearby
> [formerly in Talmage, near Ukiah]… Ka-ko pi-tum was afraid. The
> voices were insistent. After her grandfather's death (1936), she gathered
> courage and announced herself a Ma-tu…[9]

Fellow weaver and healer Salome Alcantra acknowledged Nora Cooper as
"a medicine lady, a sucking lady. She draws it out by mouth, the
pains…"[10] Keith Pike describes the respect his grandmother commanded
even outside her own community:

> Whenever they had roundhouse ceremonies, my grandmother could go
> in each roundhouse; she had a special place… She was like the reigning
> spiritual person and moved around in different places, which is unusual
> because each tribe had their own family control the roundhouses. My
> grandmother had enough respect that she could go in and out of them,
> plus she was asked by other tribes to heal them.[11]

Wala-Wala

(c. 1862–?)

Despite the efforts of several researchers, the biography of this weaver—the creator of one of the outstanding baskets in the Allen Collection—still is neither clear nor complete. There are several important clues to her identity. According to the 1880 census, an 18-year-old recorded as "Walla Walla" lived in the Sanel township near Hopland south of Ukiah. According to the census, Wala-Wala was living with her father, Captain Charley, her mother, Cha ah dum, and her brother, Che chu aro. Although she is listed as a married woman, no record of her husband appears in the family names.

Weaver Laura Somersal and artist Kathleen Smith believe that "Grandma Smith," first wife of William (Bill) Smith Sr. of Bodega Bay, also was known as Wala-Wala. Kathleen Smith, a direct descendant of the Bodega Bay Smiths, a weaver, and a cultural historian, believes that Wala-Wala was originally from Healdsburg. Laura Somersal recalled:

> She spoke the same languages as my mother [Mary John Eli, Wappo, from Geyserville, Sonoma County]. She spoke Spanish, too. I was about [a] teenager at the time, I guess... Mama would talk about her. I knew her brother, Marion Miranda... She lived with my mama's cousin before... She was real old... [12]

The basket by Wala-Wala, an unusual design woven in bulrush and embellished with abalone and clamshell disk beads, commands attention and respect for its beauty. Many who see it feel its power.

Wala-Wala, ceremonial basket, late 19th century (EA #131)

Mrs. Allen purchased the basket in 1924 from Mr. Gamble of Hopland. It was said to have been in the Gamble family for about fifty years. Mrs. Gamble told the young Elsie that the weaver was Wala-Wala, the wife of David Perry, and a medicine woman who used the basket in her doctoring. Elsie was told never to copy the design, and in her book, she admonishes the reader: "... it is taboo or forbidden for a Pomo to copy a Medicine Woman's designs..."[13]

Salome Alcantra, basket tray, n.d. (EA #125)

"Traditionally many Pomo weavers incorporated the *dau,* or spirit door, into the basket by making a break in each band of design. The *dau* allows the spirit to enter the basket and no bad thoughts or feelings to be trapped."

—Susan Billy[14]

Salome Bartlett Alcantra

(*1909–1991*)

Salome Bartlett Alcantra was the daughter of Maude Donohue (Scott) and Jim Bartlett of the Yokayo Rancheria. She describes her birthplace at a family camp next to the Russian River:

> One day we were coming from Hopland, my mother... and I... She said, "That's where you were born." Then she went over... I was just sitting driving the car, you know, the Model T... "Where?" I said. "Where those basket willows are growing there"... It grew off the bunches that my grandfather [probably Jack Donohue] picked and made a sort of a hut out of it for summer camps. You know it's too hot to live out here [on the higher ground at Yokayo], so they go down there next to the river, close to the water. Then I knew for the first time where I was born.[15]

The young Salome spent many of her childhood days with her maternal grandmother, Sally Donohue, while her mother did domestic work for various ranchers up and down the Ukiah Valley. She learned to weave from her grandmother by watching and staying close to her side. Mrs. Alcantra recalls her grandparents doing business with Grace and John Hudson:

> My grandmother used to sell [to the Hudsons]... They used to come and my grandmother used to make packing baskets for them... the cone shape... and my grandfather made [a robe] with the rabbit skin... [16]

Salome Bartlett married Joaquin Cy Alcantra of Tomales Bay, with whom she had four children. She lived twenty-seven years in Sonoma County

Salome Alcantra, Yokayo Rancheria, 1964. Marion Steinbach, photographer

"Her basketmaking was more like a spiritual thing."

—Delvin Holder[17]

Salome Alcantra, canoe basket, 1978
(EA #49)

"She [Salome] brought it out when
we were working digging roots…
That's when I saw it, a nice big one.
I liked the design on it."
—Laura Somersal[18]

before returning to the Yokayo Rancheria. Mrs. Alcantra continued to
weave, and as a grandmother was called to be a healer:

> When it was starting on me… I just did what it told me… It used to
> make me go round and round the house, round and round, so many
> times every morning before sunrise. Then one day, it took me, it told
> me to walk up the hill where we live… I just listen… It was water
> running… it was going over the rocks and it made funny rippling
> sounds… pretty sounds… real sounds… that was Indian songs, and the
> Indian medicine song… I know that it was giving me a job… when
> they call me, then to go and help them… so people come and get me.[19]

Over time, Salome Alcantra became a respected medicine woman, who
used a basket in her healing work. Fellow weaver Laura Somersal of Dry
Creek recalled:

> I took my niece Myrtle [McKay Chavez] to her one time… She couldn't
> use her hand. I took her to Salome and now she can weave again…
> That's how strong Salome is.[20]

Delvin Holder, Mrs. Alcantra's son-in-law, explains how spiritual power
guided Salome's basketweaving:

> Her basketmaking was more like a spiritual thing. Some of the
> basketmakers are like that, and that's why she had to make three at a
> time, because she wanted to be doing certain things at certain times
> [according to] spiritual instructions.[21]

Salome Alcantra died in 1991. In an interview just prior to her death, she
provided many of the details incorporated in this publication about
specific baskets in the Allen Collection, the weavers themselves, and the
preparation of basket materials.[22] Ten years younger than Elsie Allen,
Salome Alcantra was, nonetheless, a member of the turn-of-the-century
generation of weavers who did so much to sustain the vitality of Pomo
basketweaving traditions.

Maude Donohue Scott
(1884–1945)

Maude Donohue was the daughter of Sally and Jack Donohue of Yokayo Rancheria. She and her first husband, Frank Marando, had two sons, James and Elmer. Later, she married Jim Bartlett. Bartlett was well known for his leadership role in the 1869–70 acquisition of land near the Talmage Bridge for the Northern Pomo group that eventually became primary residents of the Guidiville Rancheria. The Bartletts had two children: weaver and healer Salome Alcantra, and a son, Hastings.

Maude worked for ranchers along the Ukiah Valley, washing clothes and picking hops during the harvest season. She probably learned to weave from her mother, Sally Donohue, who was also Salome Alcantra's teacher. After Jim Bartlett's death, Maude Bartlett married Dan Scott, a Kashaya Pomo, in about 1920. Their daughter Dorene Scott Mitchell recalls accompanying her mother on root-gathering trips:

> The best basket roots came from behind the Cloverdale Rancheria. Before the lumber company went in, we could just go there and pull the roots easily out of the sand. I remember my mother going up behind Yokayo where there was an eternal spring. She got really nice white-roots [sedge] up there, but it was very hard to dig them out of the dirt.[23]

Maude Scott, cooking basket, n.d. (EA #127)

This basket is an example of what Elsie Allen refers to as the "lost weave," a twining technique that involves interweaving an extra willow shoot that renders the design invisible on the inside of the basket. Elsie regretted that she had not learned the technique and could not pass down this weave to Susan Billy.[24]

Frank Miller's aunt, work basket (sifter), c.1900 (EA #20)

Frank Miller's Aunt

Honoring the Anonymous Native Artist

◆◆◆◆◆◆◆◆◆◆◆◆◆◆◆◆◆◆◆◆◆◆◆◆◆◆◆

The Elsie Allen Collection is unique among museum and private collections of Native American art in general, and baskets in particular. Most works held in these collections are, at best, documented to tribe, ethnic group, or community—only rarely to the artist who conceived and created them. The reasons for this oversight are varied and complex. One may be the challenge of the medium itself: unlike a ceramic pot, a sculpture, or a canvas, a basket does not lend itself to the recording of the identity of its maker without violating the integrity of the design. And, there have been many Indian artists who did not seek recognition. Indeed, while some became adept at playing by the rules of the art-and-craft market, others resisted it, shielding themselves and their families from the stress of becoming active players in this tough, high-stakes market economy.

These factors do not fully explain the anonymity of countless weavers whose baskets were purchased by collectors, agents, and middlemen active from the latter part of the 19th century to the Depression. Few weavers received specific recognition, even when their baskets were acquired for museum collections. The works of these nameless weavers routinely were and still are displayed in museums across the country simply as "Pomo, late 19th Century," or perhaps "Pomo, Ukiah area, c.1920." There are rare exceptions, such as Mary and William Benson, the acclaimed weavers from the Yokayo Rancheria, or Central Pomo basketmaker Joseppa Dick. In the eyes of collectors of the Arts and Crafts Movement, the names of these artists enhanced the value and collectibility of their very fine work.

It is true that many turn-of-the-century dealer-collectors with access to native weavers sought to "protect their sources" in a highly competitive market by not revealing the weavers' names or where they lived. Yet, it is not difficult to see a darker side to this pervasive tendency to overlook the individual stories of people who have been forcibly "colonized" in this country's history. Indeed, because Indian handwork, no matter how aesthetically and technically sophisticated, generally is seen as folk art, it is viewed as an expression of group identity and values, rather than of a personal artistic vision. In a hierarchical world view that mitigates against individual recognition, folk art is placed beneath the work of artists trained in the formal Western tradition. Objects are taken out of their social contexts; the historical knowledge and highly-developed skills of the individuals who made them can be inferred, but not credited.

What if the collector is herself a Native American artist, with a clear understanding of her own educational role? As demonstrated in this catalog and in the *Remember Your Relations* exhibition, a great strength of the Elsie Allen Collection is the extent of its documentation to individual weavers. According to interviews with family members, most of these women were somehow connected to Mrs. Allen or her mother through the bonds of friendship and/or kinship.

Mrs. Allen was willing to work with researchers and students who helped her to record the stories of the individual baskets in her collection. Elsie Allen's collaboration with Marion Steinbach, Susan Billy, John Pryor, and others made it possible for the Grace Hudson Museum to depart from the more common, object-based approach and focus the exhibition on the women who made these baskets. The research in the Elsie Allen Collection is ongoing, and depends on the good will of many people, particularly descendants of the weavers.

"Frank Miller's Aunt," the creator of a twined pepperwood nut basket (EA# 20), who remains nameless even in the Elsie Allen Collection, symbolizes the work still to be done—particularly oral histories. Research to date reveals the following: Frank Miller lived in Pinoleville, just north of Ukiah, because he is so identified in a photograph from the Hudson Museum Collection (Accession No. 15372); one of his children was Stella Miller Wright, also of Pinoleville. Frank Miller appears in a large group portrait of the Indian parishioners of St. Mary of the Angels Church in Ukiah, dated c.1923.

But who was his aunt? The anonymity of Frank Miller's aunt serves an important purpose. It reminds us all of a shared responsibility to document the family, local, and community history all around us. Simple actions can make the difference between anonymity and recognition, between rootlessness and having a past: names, dates, and places noted on family photographs; letters and family documents saved and safely stored; objects labeled when their makers did not think to do themselves justice. Remember Frank Miller's aunt.

Future Harvest

Environment, Basket Plants, and the Vitality of Tradition

◆◆◆◆◆◆◆◆◆◆◆◆◆◆◆◆◆◆◆◆◆◆◆◆◆◆◆◆◆

The sedge roots are hard to find now in quantity or of good quality because they have been disturbed by too many roads and buildings, but man needs to learn that the sedge root is a vital part of the harmony of nature and preserving of the soil. It is especially useful in preventing creek banks from washing away, and can be encouraged to grow by all property owners. Digging of the roots, when correctly done and leaving behind about half of those found, actually strengthens the growth and soil-holding properties of the roots... People who have land where sedge roots grow can allow basketweavers to gather roots... Please let local Indians... know if you have land that might be used for root gathering.[1]—Elsie Allen

Despite the benefits, Allen found it difficult to convince public and private land owners to let her dig. Once, she and a companion were chased away from a park for digging root. That same fall, the creek they had been chased away from was dredged and the root was covered with four feet of gravel, which completely destroyed the bed.[2]
—Beverly R. Ortiz

The premise of the original *Remember Your Relations* exhibition (1993) seemed simple, even elegant: the Elsie Allen Collection includes baskets by at least 26 individual, identified native weavers. From the outset, the focus was on these women as human beings, rather than on the

Pomo weavers gathered at Warm Springs Dam site, Sonoma County (1979), where they consulted with the Army Corps of Engineers on transplantation of sedge for weavers' continued use. (L–R): Laura Somersal, Myrtle McKay Chavez, Lynn Cannon, Elsie Allen, Lucy Smith, Josephine Wright, Mabel McKay, and Joan Dempsey with her son Damien Dempsey. Rob Botier, photographer

"Basketweaving needs dedication and interest and increasing skill and knowledge; it needs feeling and love and honor for the great weavers of the past who showed us the way."—Elsie Allen[3]

Elsie Allen cutting willow at Warm Springs Dam site, Sonoma County, 1980.
Scott M. Patterson, photographer

"She [Elsie] always had a little pick and a pruning shear in the trunk. If she'd
see something, like from here [Santa Rosa] to Sebastopol, she'd yell, 'Stop
here, stop here!' And we'd stop and she'd run off and cut things…"
—Genevieve Allen Aguilar[4]

undisputed beauty of their work, as is much more customary in museum exhibitions of native weaving.

In the course of doing research interviews on the lives of the weavers, family members talked of how essential basketmaking was in the past, and remains today, not simply a response to necessity, but a true touchstone of Pomo identity. An important theme began to emerge during discussions of the problems faced by contemporary practitioners and aspiring weavers seeking to carry on this great artistic tradition. While it only could be suggested in the original exhibition, this theme was explored in depth in the public programs that accompanied the exhibition: the greatest threat to the future of traditional basketweaving in northern California (and throughout the state) is, in fact, the effect of the loss of stewardship over land that supports plants needed by Pomo and other native peoples in order to weave—principally willow (*Salix* spp.), sedge (*Carex* spp.), bulrush (*Scirpus maritimus* and *S. pacificus*), and redbud *(Cercis occidentalis)*.[5]

This threat contrasts sharply with the widely-held and chronically-reiterated assumption that the technical and artistic knowledge of weaving itself is in jeopardy. For over one hundred years, newspaper headlines have proclaimed the death of basket-weaving with the passing of each prominent elder. It is indeed true that a handful of twining techniques no longer are practiced, but there is no real danger to the survival of the overall tradition on the North Coast—thanks to the quiet efforts of many individuals (including Elsie Allen and others represented in this collection) who continue to teach, and the growing cooperation of museums holding historic collections of baskets. In fact, better communication between weavers and curatorial staff at many northern California museums has helped forge a partnership that gives native weavers access to baskets for research and possible re-creation, including those done with so-called "lost" techniques. In the course of these exchanges, the museum benefits greatly from the expert observations of the weavers, enhancing the level of documentation of the collection, while honoring the memory of many named and still-unnamed weavers.

Sedge bed near Largo, Mendocino County, 1981. Scott M. Patterson, photographer

"[Annie Lake] wanted to get stuff to make some baskets. I said, 'Where do you go?,' and she says, 'Not too far, down on the road on the other side of the river'... We drove down toward Largo and she says, 'This is a good place—right here.' So we stopped the car and went off and down... by the river. There was a sandy place down there [with a] plant [that] sends out runners... we went and dug some of those things there and got them."
—Dr. Robert Withrow[6]

The impact of the loss of stewardship, however, is very real and its consequences serious for the vitality of tradition. In the worst cases, such as the one described by Beverly Ortiz above, there is wholesale destruction of basket plant habitat, particularly in sensitive riparian environments. Even where habitats have survived, loss of access to traditional gathering places results in degradation of the quality of weaving materials, either through neglect or abuse. One form of abuse is the application of herbicides and pesticides on both public and private lands, creating often invisible hazards for weavers.

Russian River, Ukiah Valley looking north, Mendocino County, 1981. Scott M. Patterson, photographer

"Elsie and I regularly would go and harvest sedge on the Navarro River. We also harvested on the Russian River. The Russian River roots are a lot thicker... Those are really good for the big work baskets. Over on the Navarro... are smaller roots... they are preferred for the finest coiled baskets."—Susan Billy[11]

The land has been dramatically changed. Valleys where there were homes, camping grounds and whole villages... have been flooded. Or the land has been re-sown, the walking paths paved over into highways that bypass orchards and hop fields. When Mollie Jackson looked down over the Ukiah Valley fifty years ago, it was a different sight. The places of willow, sedge grass, and redbud were guaranteed year after year. Now it is not only difficult to find new growth, but exhausting for the old women to think of traveling to unknown areas.[7]—Sandra Corrie Newman

Today, many private landowners and public lands managers simply do not know that the regular harvesting of roots and shoots of basket plants does no harm, but actually stimulates quality growth. They also may be unaware of the cultural and spiritual "rules" governing the use of basket plants that ensure preservation and improvement of the resource.

From birth to death, baskets have been an intrinsic part of traditional Indian life. We need the plants to make the baskets, and when we use them, we honor them. We take care of them, and thank them, and give back to them. When we honor the plants we honor our ancestors. When we make the baskets, we keep our connection to the past alive for the future.[8]—Linda Yamane

Other landowners, probably now a minority, oppose native access to their property because they assume that harvesters will engage in irresponsible behavior and fear they may create a legal liability.

One white gentleman came and told me I should not do it because it would destroy a lot of plants. He did not understand that I knew very well that the cutting out of roots and trimming of shrubs actually helped spread the growth and there was no danger as long as the digging and cutting was not overdone in any one place.[9]—Elsie Allen

See, they don't allow us to walk in their fields, now, to dig roots, they don't care for [them]; the cows can eat it, the horses can eat roots. It just messes their trees up and they don't like for Indians to dig their ground up.[10]
—Salome Alcantra

As this environmental concern came to the fore in interview after interview, it became clear that a full explanation of the problem went beyond the obvious effect of the legal and ideological concept of private property on North Coast geography. At the most fundamental level, the problem seems to be one of world view. Today, as we approach the

21st century, we still are haunted by beliefs shaped in another America. To the developing national imagination of the 19th century, the West was an empty land, a "wilderness" untouched by human hands. From the early years of California statehood to the closing of the frontier (1850–1870s), this Western wilderness generally was seen as the province of nature itself, a grand and glorious frontier, there to be claimed and domesticated to the uses deemed legitimate by whites: settlement, agriculture, mining, and the development of a national infrastructure of roads and railroads.

There was no place in this dichotomous scheme for subtlety or complexity. Because most Native Americans did not *appear* to practice agriculture in a way that was recognizable to whites, there also was no place for Indians, whom the brash newcomers to California contemptuously dubbed "Diggers." Nor, as a consequence, was there understanding, let alone appreciation, of the deep knowledge of the natural world carried by the Indian people whose connection to the land dates

Above, right: Elsie Allen sorting sedge roots, Warm Springs Dam site, Sonoma County, 1980. Scott M. Patterson, photographer

Right: Lucy Smith digging sedge. Scott M. Patterson, photographer

back millennia. Over a hundred years later, much of our thinking still reflects this simplistic dichotomy. Mainstream environmentalism, its roots lying in 19th century Romanticism, fails to make a place for the native view that man lives holistically and reciprocally within nature—not apart from it. It is no small irony that contemporary environmentalists have been slow to acknowledge the Native American role in creating and actively managing the "wild" landscapes we cherish as a nation.

California Indians were among those native peoples most blessed by their environment. With a generally benign climate, adequate water, and an abundant supply of useful plants, the lands in what are now Sonoma, Mendocino, and Lake Counties were occupied by the Pomo peoples. Every material need could be met with local or regional resources, the latter through an extensive North Coast trade network.

Basket materials obtained from plants growing in marshes, riverine and foothill microenvironments were gathered, prepared, and twined or coiled into baskets of great artistry and consummate utility. Traditional villages were situated close to gathering sites, where the sedge, willow, bulrush, and redbud could be cared for, their supply and consistent quality assured by practicing a range of management strategies, like selective harvesting, burning, pruning, coppicing, weeding, etc. [see Blackburn and Anderson's edited volume, *Before the Wilderness,* for a detailed discussion of these management strategies among California Indians].

> Hundreds of straight rhizomes and thousands of straight branches were needed to make the baskets produced by a single village, yet a search in the wilds for long, straight, slender switches with no lateral branching is largely in vain. In order to gather sufficient suitable branches for making the many kinds of baskets produced... in various villages, Native Americans had to manage and maintain abundant populations of certain plants at what was virtually an industrial level.[12]
>
> —Kat Anderson

Pomo basketweaving is a sophisticated, complex cultural tradition requiring a long apprenticeship within the family to achieve mastery of materials, techniques, and aesthetic design. Most baskets were and are woven by women, with a few forms (baby

baskets and some openwork baskets) made by men. All the baskets in the Elsie Allen Collection are woven ("twined") or sewn ("coiled") by women using one or more of the four principal plants used by the Pomo, in a range of techniques.

Reduced to its essentials, twining is "finger weaving," involving the twisting of pliable wefts (often sedge) around more rigid willow warps, the latter radiating like spokes from a "start." Coiling is very different: a foundation of one or three willow shoots is literally built in a continuous spiral, one layer upon the other to form the base, and then the walls and rim. This foundation is sewn together using a bone or metal awl and pliable sedge root. Redbud and bulrush are often used to create the designs. In addition, the three-rod or "three-stick" coiled baskets can be decorated with feathers, while the one-rod or "one-stick" baskets can be sewn with beads. Baby baskets made for carrying very young children are neither twined nor coiled, but made of creek dogwood tied together with cotton string (traditionally the string was made with milkweed or other natural fibers).

Willow shoots and sedge roots (technically

Opposite, left: Laura Somersal weaving a fish trap, using unpeeled willow harvested in the fall (the traditional material for work baskets).
Opposite, right: Laura Somersal twining a basket, Dry Creek Rancheria.
Above: Laura Somersal, Lucy Smith, and other workers harvest sedge at the Warm Springs Dam site.
Right: Laura Somersal coiling a one-stick basket, Dry Creek Rancheria.

All photos by Scott M. Patterson, Sonoma County, 1980.

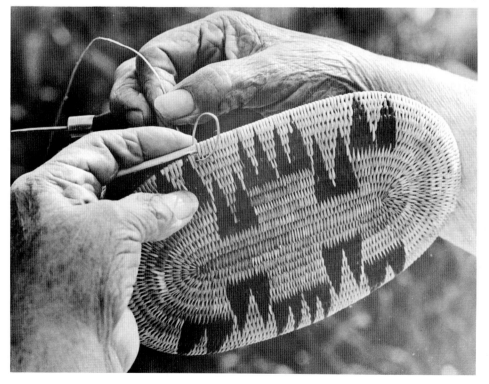

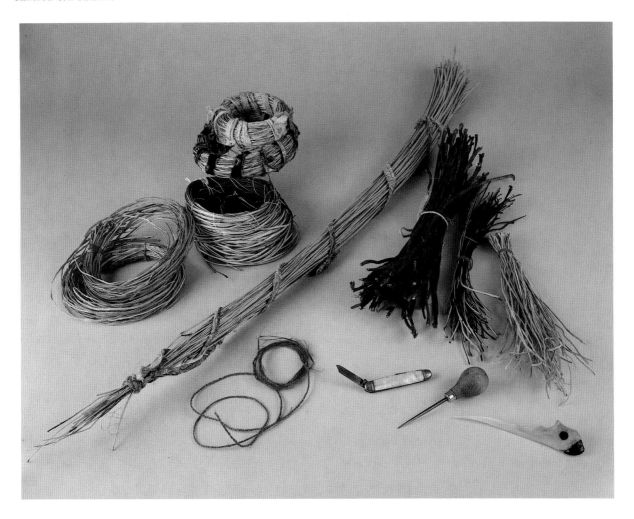

Basketmaking plant materials and tools (clockwise from left): sedge root coils;
redbud coil; willow bundle; unpeeled bulrush bundle; prepared and split bulrush;
sedge root bundle; deer bone awl made for fine coiled work; large awl used on
twined work baskets; pocketknife; and milkweed, the traditional "string" used in
baby baskets.

"The knife is used for thinning out the back of the roots and scraping the
willow and for starting the split when you've gathered roots... if you need to
narrow down the root to match your other roots or just to make a finer root,
then definitely you are going to use your knife... The original awl was a bone
from the front leg of a deer. It's a bone that's almost shaped like an awl when it
comes off the deer, although it's very long, so we do trim it down. In time, it
breaks when you use it... but you can resharpen it."—Susan Billy[13]

rhizomes)—both of which grow long and straight in well-managed habitats—provide the basic structure of the Pomo basket.

> All the basic foundations of the baskets are the gray willow [or] white willow... [it] is used for all the coiling and all the rough baskets, work-type baskets... There were two different harvests—a spring harvest when you gather before the leaves start to bud out and the skin comes off fairly easily... and is used for the foundation... The other harvest is in the fall. That's when you want to leave the bark on because once the leaves bud out... and they fall off there are little nodules along the willow and it's quite rough... Usually when you see a work-type basket that's a dark color with the bark on, that is from a fall harvest... it's more bumpy because the leaves grew.

> Elsie and I harvested willow along the Russian River. We went up near Lake Pillsbury... There are also some stands in Lake County...

> The main material for all the coil work is sedge root... when we harvest... we dig around the plant to find that runner... You

Kathleen Smith harvesting bulrush, 1994. Beverly R. Ortiz, photographer

"My black trim in my baskets is a root. I search well the waters where I note slough grass [bulrush] standing. I must follow the grass stems down into the mire and work loose the roots."—Annie Burke[14]

Kathleen Smith cutting redbud, El Portal, Mariposa County, 1991. Beverly R. Ortiz, photographer

"The red decoration in the pattern of my baskets is the natural coloring of the bark covering the twigs of redbud... These I must cut from the tree when they are yet very young and tender, then split them with my teeth to break them into little strands which are also wound into coils for drying."—Annie Burke[15]

want the longest roots you can find... The longer the root, the more weaving material you have that's going to be uniform.

Elsie and I regularly would go and harvest sedge on the Navarro River. We also harvested on the Russian River. The Russian River roots are a lot thicker... Those are really good for the big work baskets. Over on the Navarro... are smaller roots... they are preferred for the finest coiled baskets. [16]—Susan Billy

Dyed bulrush root ("black root") and redbud shoots provide the characteristic black and reddish-brown designs in both coiled and twined baskets.

Bulrush... do not grow very long... 12-14 inches is a good size root... It is the runner... we cut... and the plant makes more... The bulrush grows quite dark or black, dark brown... it's not always uniform... [so] we do dye [it] to even out the color. The old ladies used a recipe of black walnut husks and... sometimes they'd mix blue clay and they always used rain water... wood ashes... old rusty nails... They'd use a galvanized tub... big enough for the roots and you make up this muck and stuff your roots down... and you'd just let them sit in there... anywhere from 3 to 4 weeks to 2 to 3 months... You want to split them after they've been dyed.

The redbud... is harvested in winter after a hard frost... What you want... is that red bark attached to the wood... [it] is so thick that we'd split it in half again, throwing away that inside portion... But it's not just the bark you're after, the bark has to be still attached to the wood for it to have that strength... You work it down as close as you can to how you're going to weave with it, except, you never do your final trimming for any materials until you're actually ready to weave... Elsie and I always used to go over to Lake County for the redbud; although it grows around here in the Ukiah Valley, it doesn't really make the red bark—it's very gray for the most part around here.[17]—Susan Billy

For each of the plants, there is the right time for harvesting, and the right process—from a few months to a year—for preparing the material for basketmaking.

Other natural decorative materials, such as abalone shell, clamshell disk beads, and various feathers also must be obtained and prepared for use through traditional processes. In the case of clamshell disk beads, usually manufactured by men, this is particularly laborious. Even when using another innovation, purchased glass or (rarely) ceramic beads, to create the spectacular coiled baskets that have found a ready market since the late 19th century, the process of individually attaching each bead in a striking overall design requires great skill. Examples of the principal techniques of harvesting plant materials and basketmaking are shown in the accompanying photographs.

Above: Annie Lake, beaded baskets (L–R, Rear: EA #62, 61; Middle: #65, 67, 69;
Front: #68, 66)
Left: Annie Lake, gift basket, 1975 (EA #81)

"Then you would put this [woodpecker] trap where the hole is. Then they
would come out and go right into the trap… And the woodpeckers are… kind
of special birds. They [have] beautiful colors on them, and the Pomo people
like the feathers to decorate their baskets with, the ones that are fine weaved
baskets."—Milton "Bun" Lucas[18]

Susan Billy, Grace Hudson Museum, Ukiah, 1993. *Ukiah Daily Journal* photograph

Susan Billy poses with her "thousand stick" basket during the run of the *Remember Your Relations* exhibition in Ukiah. Elsie is holding this same basket in the photograph taken by Scott M. Patterson (1981) visible in the background.

Legacy

◆◆◆◆◆◆◆◆◆◆◆◆◆◆◆◆◆◆◆◆◆◆◆

The Elsie Allen Collection is unique among existing museum collections of Pomo baskets: the Allen Collection was initiated, developed, and preserved by native weavers themselves. Two Pomo women, Annie Burke and Elsie Allen, assembled this historic collection over a period of more than forty years. From the 1940s into the 1980s, small audiences learned about Pomo baskets and caught a glimpse of traditional Pomo culture through the efforts of this mother and daughter.

In the 1940s and 1950s, Elsie Allen and her mother often went together to fairs and community centers to exhibit the collection, and to demonstrate their love of basketweaving to Indians and non-Indians alike. Even when she did not weave, in the years when she was raising her family, Elsie Allen was an active member of the Pomo Indian Women's Club, chairing the basket committee.

In 1962, Elsie Allen decided to take her mother's dedication to preserving Pomo basketry one step further: she began teaching basketry to anyone who showed an interest. In so doing, she encountered much criticism from within the Pomo community. Interestingly, the criticism came from both traditionalist and progressive quarters. There were—and are—those who feel that she went too far in her willingness to share special knowledge with a wide public, and there were also those who felt that perpetuating such traditions was antithetical to native prospects for successful adaptation to a white world. This is what Elsie Allen had to say about this issue:

> Some of my Pomo people were not pleased with me for doing this and even some of my own family came to me and told me I should stop doing it. They felt these old ways should die and we should forget the past heritage... I felt very strongly that my people who opposed my basketmaking were wrong and were letting fears overcome their better sense, as how could we ever bring back an understanding of our own background and the beautiful things our old people did if we did not revive some of these arts?[1]

She persevered, teaching formal classes to small groups and taking individual students of unusual promise and dedication, like Susan Billy and Marion Steinbach. Mrs. Steinbach's deep interest contributed so much to the documentation of the Allen Collection:

> I remember Elsie being so willing to share everything she knew. There were no "secrets" as some weavers lead you to believe... Elsie

Genevieve Aguilar with part of the family collection. She is wearing the family's valuable clamshell beads and holding the basket made by her great-grandmother Mary Arnold, 1940

"People were curious as to why she [Annie Burke] didn't have any baskets to show... They liked her weaving. They liked her work... So then she got together with my mother [Elsie Allen] and they started holding on to the things they made, plus adding to it [including] other people's [basketweaving] which has increased the collection. It was really my grandma that got that started."—Genevieve Allen Aguilar[2]

Elsie Allen, baby basket, n.d. (EA #19)

Elsie Allen made this fine cradle basket to carry her grandson David Aguilar.

was a natural teacher. She was soft-spoken, slow moving, thorough, encouraging... I was her first student to ever complete a basket.[3]

Another of Elsie Allen's non-Indian students, Paula Fugman, reflected:

> She [Elsie] actually I think understood that white culture learns and is very verbal and does things very differently. And she was really a transitional person... when she accepted you and she called you hers, then it felt very easy to trust her methods.[4]

Over the years, Elsie Allen taught many students the basics of Pomo basketweaving—from the gathering and preparation of sedge, willow, and redbud to the completion of a basket and its long-term care. Like any true elder, she also shared the wisdom that she had gained during her long life

with her younger students, including Paula Fugman:

> I think what she taught me is that you have to make your own life... I felt like my whole soul was sort of showing because she would talk about the eye of the basket reflecting the state of mind of the person at the moment they did it... She just knew a lot and wanted to share a lot... [she] sort of led you gently with humorous things into finding things or figuring out things... she was a Socratic kind of teacher.[5]

Elsie Allen also shared her love of weaving with countless thousands on the many occasions when she demonstrated and exhibited the collection—such as when she was invited to the Festival of American Folklife on the Washington Mall (1974), or Hunter College in New York (1983). Her granddaughter, Linda Aguilar McGill, remembers:

> She was invited to Washington, D.C., to participate in an International Awareness Day, and she was able to identify and help label baskets [at the Smithsonian Institution]... As a senior citizen, she was driving to San Francisco doing seminars at the age of 70. She was never home. She was... kind of a basketweaving social butterfly, if you will, in terms of really going wherever the need or desire was to learn.[6]

One of the most important relationships reflected in the collection is the nearly twenty years' association with her relative and student, Susan Billy:

> I hitchhiked up [to Ukiah] from Hopland and I knocked on her door. I said, "You don't know me, but I'm your relative. Ignatius is my father. I'm Susan Billy. All my life my Daddy told me that you could answer some questions for me about the baskets. I would like to learn how to make the baskets..." She was kind of stunned for a moment. Then she invited me in...

> Her first question was, "Why do you want to learn this? Nobody wants to learn this anymore." ... I began to just literally sit at her feet until my daughter [Dawn] was born... Elsie pretty much just let me ask all the questions. And I asked a lot of questions. We also spent a lot of quiet time just *working*. Elsie is a very humble person... when I started, she would always just show me. She would

say, "This is how I do this." She wouldn't say, "This is how *you* should do this." ... She let me find my own way, within the work.[7]

Following her great-aunt's lead, Susan has assumed a teaching role in the community, and she continues to bring Pomo weaving into the public eye. She entertains and enriches students, from local schoolchildren to film and television audiences, with stories of Elsie Allen as she shares what she learned about Pomo traditions from this consummate teacher. "My hope," she explains, "is that I, too, might be able to share what I have learned from Elsie... that Creator will help me, in these busy, busy days, to find the time to sit quietly and simply weave."

Susan Billy and Elsie Allen often traveled together, sometimes to nearby spots in Mendocino or Lake County to gather willow or redbud, and sometimes as far away as New York, to demonstrate and talk about weaving. Susan Billy describes Elsie Allen's work as a consultant:

> She had been invited by the Museum of the American Indian and the Museum of Natural History to come in and look at their collection in storage to see if she could identify anything, and she was able to identify several baskets either by the actual weaver or the area where it came from, and that was absolutely fascinating to me. She could look at the knot

or the way the pattern was... or just little intricacies, and she could identify the weaver.[8]

The relationship between Elsie Allen and Susan Billy endured. This catalog, and the exhibition which it accompanies, are in large measure a reflection of the bond between Elsie Allen, the teacher, and Susan Billy, her student.

The teaching collection itself remained fluid. While she kept her mother's baskets and contributed many of her own, Elsie also collected from other weavers, often through trade or purchase. The collection grew to include baskets by many of the weavers of her generation, and to reflect the complex network of kinship and friendship in which Elsie lived. It is this wide and deep network of human relationships that made *Remember Your Relations* possible.

When Elsie Allen fell ill in the late 1980s her daughter, Genevieve Allen Aguilar, accepted the collection and its legacy as her responsibility. The audience for the collection expanded with Mrs. Aguilar's decision to share it first with museums in Mendocino County and then with the Oakland Museum of California.

Although she is not a weaver herself, Genevieve Allen Aguilar accompanied her mother on many educational trips, as Elsie had done with her mother. Through these experiences, Genevieve

Susan Billy, coiled baskets, 1975, 1976
(L: first basket; R: first feathered basket)

"My first feathered basket, I carried... around with me for months before giving it to my father, Ignatius."
—Susan Billy[9]

Five generations in Elsie Allen's family, 1990. Front (L–R): Elsie Allen, great-great granddaughter Alyssa Parker, and great-granddaughter Darla Parker. Rear (L–R): granddaughter Linda Aguilar McGill, daughter Genevieve Allen Aguilar. Dugan Aguilar, photographer

Dugan, nephew of Elsie's son-in-law Ralph Aguilar, recalls that Elsie, who couldn't speak due to a stroke, and the baby "were really connecting without talking... [they were] touching hands."[10]

learned about the power of Pomo baskets and their value as a teaching tool.

> I've seen other baskets... The [Pomo] work is beautiful and the workmanship is just like no other... I don't want the culture to fade... By exhibiting the baskets... I think it will continue.[11]

As a way to preserve the cultural legacy of Pomo basketry, Genevieve Aguilar and her family made a loan of her mother's collection to the Mendocino County Museum in Willits, California in 1988. In accordance with the family's wishes, the museum developed the long-term exhibition, *A Promise Kept*, showing many of the 131 baskets in the Elsie Allen Collection.

In 1992, Genevieve Aguilar agreed to exhibiting approximately ninety of the baskets in Ukiah, Elsie Allen's adoptive home town, in a temporary exhibition at the Grace Hudson Museum. The Hudson Museum originated a new show, *Remember Your Relations: The Elsie Allen Baskets, Family & Friends*, to acknowledge explicitly the complex ties of family and community reflected in

the collection's composition. The show, co-curated by Hudson Museum staff with weaver Susan Billy, met with tremendous success, enjoying attendance and support from San Francisco to Humboldt County.

With then-Director Pete Passoff, Plant Science Advisor Glenn McGourty, and Staff Forester Greg Giusti of the University of California Cooperative Extension for Mendocino County, Hudson Museum staff developed two public programs to focus on the environmental context of the weaving tradition. *Native American Plant Collecting & Natural Resource Management* and *Future Harvest: Native Weavers, Basket Plants & Public Lands* addressed issues such as the diminishing habitats of basketry plants and the problems that weavers have getting access to them on both private and publicly held lands.

In 1988, upon making the loan of the collection to the Mendocino County Museum, Genevieve Aguilar expressed her hope that the family collection would have an ongoing and widespread impact. The enthusiastic public response to the

Elsie Allen High School, 1995. H.P. Thoeni, photographer

1993 Hudson Museum programs and exhibit led her to collaborate on a Bay Area exhibition of *Remember Your Relations* at the Oakland Museum of California. With the Oakland Museum exhibition, publication of this catalog in collaboration with Heyday Books, and the accompanying programs, classes, and workshops, we hope that Mrs. Aguilar's wish has indeed been fulfilled.

Late in 1992, Elsie Allen's role as an educator in her community was acknowledged in yet another way. The Santa Rosa School Board selected Elsie

Allen's name—she edged out writer Jack London for the honor—for a new high school. Dan Shay, a member of St. Rose Church, where Elsie Allen was baptized, nominated the basketweaver and teacher to "offer a proud reminder to all… of the enduring values of our first Americans." Members of the Allen family, friends, students, teachers, school officials, and community members came together on November 15, 1994 to dedicate Elsie Allen High School. Assistant Principal Pam Devlin explained, "She was a teacher. She was a lifelong learner, and we look to her for those values."

The hands of Elsie Allen and Susan Billy, 1987. Jean McMann, Photographer

September 22 was Elsie's birthday. I visited her grave. I brought her a rose and I cried. I sure do love that woman! And I sure do miss her. I can still hear her beautiful laugh, see her eyes sparkle.

She gave me a lot! Oh—not material things—but special direction for my life. An answer to the calling in my heart. She gave me purpose and a doorway through which to walk. She taught me courage and respect.

Creating life, each day—making our existence through our hands, hearts and thoughts… experiencing the joy and sorrow and everything in between— this is the meaning of life for me.

—Susan Billy

Notes

FACING TITLE PAGE

1. Interview with Genevieve Allen Aguilar by Sandra Metzler and Dan Taylor, August 30, 1989, Collection of Mendocino County Museum, Research Box #5A-1

INTRODUCTION, pp.9–21

1. Elsie Allen, personal communication, February 13, 1982

2. Jane Babcock Akins, personal communication, 1993, Parsell Papers 1939–1948, Collection of Mendocino County Museum, Acc. #83-18-1

3. Personal communication, Parsell to Metzler, 1983, Collection of Mendocino County Museum, Acc. #83-18-1

4. Interview with Genevieve Aguilar by Sandra Metzler, July 19, 1988, Collection of Mendocino County Museum, Acc. #88-9-1

5. Elsie Allen, Pomo Basketmaking, A Supreme Art for the Weaver, 1972, pp.11-12

6. McLendon, Sally, and Brenda Shears-Holland, "The Basketmakers: The Pomoans of California." The Ancestors, Native Artists of the Americas, 1979, p.124; McLendon, Sally, "California Baskets and Basketmakers" in Meaning and Form in Native American Baskets, 1992, p.59

7. Purdy, Carl, "The Pomo Indian Baskets and Their Makers" in Out West, 1901-02, pp.38-44; McLendon and Shears-Holland, pp.113-115; Milton Lucas 1989, personal communication; McLendon 1992

8. Arlene Anderson 1987, personal communication

9. Barrett, Samuel A., Pomo Indian Basketry, 1908, p.157

10. Allen, Pomo Basketmaking, pp.51-58

11. Purdy, pp.23-25; Barrett, pp.145-157; Allen, pp.39-49; McLendon and Shears-Holland, pp.118-120; McLendon 1992, p.59; Judith Polanich 1996, personal communication

12. McLendon and Shears-Holland, p.118; McLendon 1992, p.59

13. Nicholson, Grace, "List of Indian Baskets Made by Mary and William Benson-Pomo Tribe," n.d.

14. Patterson, Scott M., A Sense of Place, California North Coast Ethnographic Photography, 1989, cover photo description

15. Purdy, pp.25-26; Barrett, pp.158-162; Allen, pp.26-36, 37-38, 58-62; Newman, Sandra Corrie, Indian Basket Weaving; How to Weave Pomo, Yurok, Pima and Navajo Baskets, 1974, pp.13-18; McLendon and Shears-Holland, p.120; Mabel McKay 1981-1987, personal communication

16. Barrett, pp.162-168

17. Kroeber, Alfred, "California Basketry and the Pomo," in American Anthropologist, 1909, p.36

18. Barrett, pp.169-172; McLendon and Shears-Holland, pp.122-123

19. Hudson, J.W., "Pomo Basket Makers," in Overland Monthly, 1893; Purdy, pp.30-38; Barrett, pp.172-276

20. Kathleen Smith, 1994, personal communication

21. McLendon and Shears-Holland, p.118; Sherrie Smith-Ferri 1996, personal communication

22. McLendon, Sally, "Pomo Baskets: The Legacy of William and Mary Benson" in Native Peoples, 1990; McLendon, Sally, "Preparing Museum Collections for Use as Primary Data in Ethnographic Research" in The Research Potential of Anthropological Museum Collections, 1981, p.208

23. Barrett, p.137

24. Purdy, pp.21-23; Barrett, pp.136-145; McLendon and Shears-Holland, p.121; Sherrie Smith-Ferri 1996, personal communication

25. Laura Somersal 1982, personal communication; Mabel McKay 1981, personal communication; Jeanne Billy 1992, personal communication; June Dollar 1994,

personal communication

26. Purdy, p.23; Barrett, pp.141-145

27. Hudson, pp.568-570; Allen, pp.18-19; Theodoratus, Dorothea J., David W. Peri, Clinton M. Blount, and Scott M. Patterson, An Ethnographic Survey of the Mahilkaune (Dry Creek) Pomo, 1975, p.176; Peri, David W., and Scott M. Patterson, "The Basket is in the Roots, That's Where it Begins" in Journal of California Anthropology, 1985, pp.21-23; Arlene Anderson 1981–83, personal communcation; Peri, David W., Scott M. Patterson, and Susan L. McMurray, The Makahmo Pomo: An Ethnographic Survey of the Cloverdale (Makahmo) Pomo, 1985, pp.73, 87-91; Ortiz, Beverly R., "Contemporary California Indian Basketweavers and the Environment," in Before the Wilderness: Environmental Management by Native Californians, 1993, pp.202-205

28. Allen, pp.19,20; Arlene Anderson 1981, personal communication

29. Newman, p.9; Arlene Anderson 1981, personal communication

30. Josephine Santos Wright 1993, personal communication; Allen, p.20

31. Allen, p.18; Mabel McKay 1991, personal communication; Arlene Anderson 1991, personal communication; Newman, pp.9,10,12

32. Julia Parker 1991, personal communication

33. Mabel McKay 1981-87, personal communication; Peri, David W. and Sally McLendon, Notes on Southern Pomo Basketry, pp. 49-51; Peri and Patterson, 1985, pp.64-66

34. Barrett, pp.171-172; Peri and McLendon, pp.16

35. Purdy, pp.321-322; Barrett, pp.170-171; Kroeber, p.242; Winther, Barbara, "Pomo Banded Baskets and Their Dau Marks" in American Indian Art, 1985, pp.50-57; Kathleen Smith 1993, personal communication

36. McLendon 1992, pp.63-64

37. Hudson 1893; McLendon and Shears-Holland, pp.111-113; McLendon 1990; McLendon, Sally, "Collecting Pomoan Baskets, 1889-1939" in *Museum Anthropology*, 1993; Smith-Ferri, Sherrie, "Basket Weavers, Basket Collectors, and the Market: A Case Study of Joseppa Dick," in *Museum Anthropology*, 1993; Smith-Ferri, Sherrie, "Webs of Meaning: Pomoan Baskets, Their Creators and Their Collectors," unpublished paper, 1990

38. Bates, Craig, "The Big Pomo Basket" in *American Indian Basketry*, 1983, pp.12-14

39. Kathleen Smith 1990, personal communication

40. Marion Steinbach 1995, personal communication

41. Bette Holmes 1993, personal communication

42. Allen, p.19; Arlene Anderson personal communication, 1981; Ortiz, Beverly R., Elsie Allen and Susan Billy in "California Indian Basketweavers Gathering, A Special Report," in *News from Native California*, p.17

43. Mason, Otis T., *Aboriginal American Basketry: Studies in a Textile Art Without Machinery*, 1972

44. Kathleen Smith 1990, personal communication

45. I would like to thank Sherrie Smith-Ferri for her meticulous review of this paper, which benefited greatly from her insights and scholarship. I would like to thank, as well, the many Pomo individuals who, since 1981, have so graciously shared their knowledge of Pomo basketry with me: Linda Aguilar McGill, Jeanne Billy, Susan Billy, June Dollar, Bonnie Elliott, Silverio Espinosa, Eleanor Gonzales, Bette Holmes, Delfina Martinez, Mabel McKay, Julia Parker, Lucy Smith, Kathleen Smith, Sherrie Smith-Ferri, Laura Somersal (1892–1990), Bernice Torrez, and Josephine Santos Wright. I would especially like to acknowledge Mabel McKay (1907–1993), who from 1981 to 1987 taught me how to make one-stick, Pomo-style coiled baskets. I would also like to acknowledge Mabel's longtime student Arlene Anderson (1931–1991), who taught me other techniques; Craig D. Bates, Curator of Ethnography at Yosemite National Park, who taught me how to make my first central California Indian-style basket; Elsie Allen, Milton "Bun" Lucas (1925–1995), and Julia F. Parker, who offered additional encouragement with my basketry; and the many non-Pomo California Indian weavers from across the state who have shared their basketry traditions with me.

ELSIE COMANCHE ALLEN, pp.22–29

1. Allen, Elsie, *Pomo Basketmaking, A Supreme Art for the Weaver*, 1972, p.15

2. Ibid., p.8

3. Ibid., p.9

4. Ibid., p.10

5. Susan Billy to Dot Brovarney, personal communication, February 1996

6. Allen, *Pomo Basketmaking*, p.13

7. Interview with Bette Holmes by Beverly R. Ortiz, August 21, 1992, in *Pomo Basketweavers: A Tribute to Three Elders*, script page 18, 1992

8. Allen, *Pomo Basketmaking*, p.14

9. Interview with Linda Aguilar McGill by David Ludwig, in Beverly R. Ortiz, August 9, 1992, *Pomo Basketweavers: A Tribute to Three Elders*, script page 23, 1992

10. Susan Billy to Dot Brovarney, personal communication, February 4, 1996

11. Susan Billy to Dot Brovarney, personal communication, 1993

12. Interview with Susan Billy by Sandra Metzler with Dot Brovarney, February 5,1989, Collection of Mendocino County Museum, Acc.#89-26-1

13. Allen, *Pomo Basketmaking*, p.14

IMMEDIATE FAMILY, pp.30–51

1. Interview with Elsie Allen by Sandra Metzler-Smith with Gerry York, October 6, 1981, Collection of Mendocino County Museum, Acc.#81-85-1

2. Allen, Elsie, *Pomo Basketmaking, A Supreme Art for the Weaver*, 1972, p.13

3. Susan Billy to Dot Brovarney, personal communication, February 4, 1996

4. Allen, *Pomo Basketmaking*, p.9

5. Allen to Metzler-Smith with York, Mendocino County Museum, Acc.#81-85-1

6. Ibid.

7. Allen, *Pomo Basketmaking*, p.13

8. Notes, 1984, Collection of The North Lake Tahoe Historical Society's Marion Steinbach Indian Basket Museum

9. Interview with Laura Somersal by Dot Brovarney, March 29, 1990, Collection of Mendocino County Museum, Acc.#90-43-1

10. According to her son John, Agnes Commache Santana and Elsie Comanche Allen spelled their father's name differently.

11. Interview with John Santana by Dot Brovarney, October 12, 1995, Collection of Grace Hudson Museum, unnumbered

12. Ibid.

13. Ibid.

14. Notes, 1984, Marion Steinbach Indian Basket Museum

15. Susan Billy to Dot Brovarney, personal communication, 1993

16. Allen to Metzler-Smith with York, Mendocino County Museum, Acc.#81-85-1. In contrast to Elsie Allen's statement, her sister-in-law, Lena Cordova Abasolo, recalls Annie Burke weaving with feathers (Abasolo to Susan Billy, personal communication, 1996)

17. Susan Billy to Dot Brovarney, personal communication, 1993

18. Interview with Susan Billy by David Ludwig, June 28, 1992, in Beverly R. Ortiz, *Pomo Basketweavers: A Tribute to Three Elders*, script pages 19-20, 1992

EXTENDED FAMILY, pp.52–57

1. Interview with Virginia Knight Buck by Sandra Metzler-Smith, 1981, Collection of the Mendocino County Museum, Acc.# 81-70-1

2. Ibid.

3. Interview with Elsie Allen by Sandra Metzler-Smith with Gerry York, October 6, 1981, Collection of Mendocino County Museum, Acc.# 81-85-1

4. Interview with Ethel Knight Burke by Dot Brovarney and Susan Billy, March 3, 1993, Collection of Grace Hudson Museum, unnumbered

5. Susan Billy to Dot Brovarney, personal communication, 1993

6. Burke to Brovarney and Billy, Collection of Grace Hudson Museum, unnumbered

7. Interview with Lois Lockart Compton by Dot Brovarney, March 19, 1993, Collection of Grace Hudson Museum, unnumbered. A branch of Gladys Lockhart's family chose to drop the "h" and spell the name Lockart.

8. Ibid.

9. Ibid.

10. Ibid.

A COHORT OF FRIENDS, pp.58–70

1 Collection of Grace Hudson Museum, #15,273

2. Evangeline Duncan to Dot Brovarney, personal communication, 1993

3. Ibid.

4. Interview with Laura Somersal by Dot Brovarney, March 29, 1990, Collection of Mendocino County Museum, Acc.#90-43-1

5. Ibid.

6. Ibid.

7. Interview with Myrtle McKay Chavez by Dot Brovarney, February 26, 1993, Collection of Grace Hudson Museum, unnumbered

8. Somersal to Brovarney, Collection of Mendocino County Museum, Acc.#90-43-1

9. Ibid.

10. Ibid.

11. Chavez to Dot Brovarney, Collection of Grace Hudson Museum, unnumbered

12. Somersal to Brovarney, Collection of Mendocino County Museum, Acc.#90-43-1

13. Chavez to Dot Brovarney, Collection of Grace Hudson Museum, unnumbered

14. Interview with Robert Jackson by Dot Brovarney, February 3, 1993, Collection of Grace Hudson Museum, unnumbered

15. Somersal to Brovarney, Collection of Mendocino County Museum, Acc.#90-43-1

16. Jackson to Brovarney, Collection of Grace Hudson Museum, unnumbered

17. Interview with Salome Alcantra by Dot Brovarney, March 30, 1990, Collection of Mendocino County Museum, Acc.#90-44-1

18. Somersal to Brovarney, Collection of Mendocino County Museum, Acc.#90-43-1

19. Jackson to Brovarney, Collection of Grace Hudson Museum, unnumbered

20. Interview with Bonnie Elliott by Dot Brovarney, March 16, 1993, Collection of Grace Hudson Museum, unnumbered

21. Interview with Susan Billy by Sandra Mezler with Dot Brovarney, August 5, 1989, Collection of Mendocino County Museum, Acc.#89-26-1

LAKE COUNTY WEAVERS, pp.71–77

1. Interview with Delvin Holder by Dot Brovarney, March 4, 1993, Collection of Grace Hudson Museum, unnumbered

2. Ibid.

3. Ibid.

4. Ibid.

5. Ibid.

6. Ibid.

7. Notes, 1984, Collection of The North Lake Tahoe Historical Society's Marion Steinbach Indian Basket Museum

HEALERS, pp. 78-87

1. Interview with Greg Sarris by David Ludwig, June 14, 1992, in Beverly R. Ortiz, *Pomo Basketweavers: A Tribute to Three Elders*, script page 31, 1992

2. Interview with Milton "Bun" Lucas by David Ludwig, July 1991, in Beverly R. Ortiz, *Pomo Basketweavers: A Tribute to Three Elders*, script page 30, 1992

3. Allen, Elsie, *Pomo Basketmaking, A Supreme Art for the Weaver*, 1972, p.8

4. Interview with Keith Pike by Dot Brovarney, March 1, 1993, Collection of Grace Hudson Museum, unnumbered

5. Interview with Salome Alcantra by Dot Brovarney, March 30, 1990, Collection of Mendocino County Museum, Acc.#90-44-1

6. Sarris, Greg, *Mabel McKay, Weaving the Dream*, 1994, p.38

7. Pike to Brovarney, Collection of Grace Hudson Museum, unnumbered

8. Ibid.

9. *"Ka-Ko Pi-Tum* (known to the whites as Nora, wife of John Cooper)" manuscript, Collection of Grace Hudson Museum, #20,227, 1936/37. The accent marks in John Hudson's manuscript have been eliminated from this version because they do not concur with current linguistic convention.

10. Alcantra to Brovarney, Collection of Mendocino County Museum, Acc.#90-44-1

11. Pike to Brovarney, Collection of Grace Hudson Museum, unnumbered

12. Interview with Laura Somersal by Dot Brovarney, March 29, 1990, Collection of Mendocino County Museum, Acc.#90-43-1

13. Allen, *Pomo Basketmaking*, p.22; notes, 1984, Collection of The North Lake Tahoe Historical Society's Marion Steinbach Indian Basket Museum

14. Susan Billy to Dot Brovarney, personal communication, 1996

15. Alcantra to Brovarney, Collection of Mendocino County Museum, Acc.#90-44-1

16. Ibid.

17. Interview with Delvin Holder by Dot Brovarney, March 4, 1993, Collection of Grace Hudson Museum, unnumbered

18. Somersal to Brovarney, Collection of Mendocino County Museum, Acc.#90-43-1

19. Alcantra to Brovarney, Collection of Mendocino County Museum, Acc.#90-44-1

20. Somersal to Brovarney, Collection of Mendocino County Museum, Acc.#90-43-1

21. Holder to Brovarney, Collection of Grace Hudson Museum, unnumbered

22. Alcantra to Brovarney, Collection of Mendocino County Museum, Acc.#90-44-1

23. Dorene Scott Mitchell to Dot Brovarney, personal communication, December 1995

24. Allen, *Pomo Basketmaking*, p.47; Interview with Susan Billy by Sandra Metzler with Dot Brovarney, August 5, 1989, Collection of Mendocino County Museum, Acc.#89-26-1

FUTURE HARVEST, pp.91–101

1. Allen, Elsie, *Pomo Basketmaking, A Supreme Art for the Weaver*, 1972, pp.19-20

2. Blackburn and Anderson, *Before the Wilderness: Environmental Management by Native Californians*, 1993, p.206

3. Allen, *Pomo Basketmaking*, p.15

4. Interview with Genevieve Allen Aguilar and Ralph Aguilar by Sandra Metzler and Dan Taylor, August 30, 1989, Collection of Mendocino County Museum, Research Box #5A-1

5. *Remember Your Relations* suggested an opportunity to build on public awareness stimulated by a 1992 public program on the contributions of American plants to world food and medicine. Moving from the hemispheric broad brush of that Columbian Quincentenary subject to the specific environments of the North Coast, and the particular case of basket plant microenvironments, museum staff developed two programs for *Remember Your Relations* with the Mendocino County Cooperative Extension Office. In these, weavers and public lands managers joined members of the general public to discuss the problems faced by anyone trying to continue to weave today. This chapter owes a great deal to the dialogue during those programs, as well as to the published scholarship of David Peri, the late Scott M. Patterson, Beverly Ortiz, and Dr. Kat Anderson, and to Dr. John W. Hudson's lifelong interest in native ethnobotany, which first brought the Hudson-Carpenter Collection to the attention of Dr. Anderson. Dr. Anderson's seminal contribution to the museum's public programs in 1992–93 is gratefully acknowledged here, as is the importance of her co-edited (with Thomas C. Blackburn) volume, *Before the Wilderness, Environmental Management by Native Californians* (Ballena Press, Menlo Park, CA, 1993).

6. Interview with Dr. Robert Withrow by Sandra Metzler, January 15, 1983, Collection of Mendocino County Museum, Acc.#83-2-1

7. Newman, Sandra Corrie, *Indian Basketweaving, How to Weave Pomo, Yurok, Pima and Navajo Baskets*, 1974, p.4

8. Keator, Glenn, Linda Yamane, and Ann Lewis, *In Full View: Three Ways of Seeing California Plants*, 1995, p.85

9. Allen, *Pomo Basketmaking*, 1972, p.14

10. Interview with Salome Alcantra by Dot Brovarney, March 30, 1990, Collection of Mendocino County Museum, Acc.#90-44-1

11. Interview with Susan Billy by Dot Brovarney, March 20, 1993, Collection of Grace Hudson Museum, unnumbered

12. Blackburn and Anderson, *Before the Wilderness*, 1993, p.162

13. Billy to Brovarney, Collection of Grace Hudson Museum, unnumbered

14. *Ukiah Daily Journal*, c.1953

15. *Ukiah Daily Journal*, c.1953

16. Billy to Brovarney, Collection of Grace Hudson Museum, unnumbered

17. Ibid.

18. Interview with Milton "Bun" Lucas by David Ludwig, July 1991, in Beverly R. Ortiz, *Pomo Basketweavers: A Tribute to Three Elders*, script page 6, 1992

LEGACY, pp.102-107

1. Allen, Elsie, *Pomo Basketmaking, A Supreme Art for the Weaver*, 1972, p.14

2. Interview with Genevieve Allen Aguilar and Ralph Aguilar by Sandra Metzler and Dan Taylor, August 30, 1989, Collection of Mendocino County Museum, Research Box 5A-1

3. Marion Steinbach to Dot Brovarney, correspondence, October 1989, Collection of Mendocino County Museum, Research Box 5A-1

4. Interview with Paula Fugman by Dot Brovarney, November 14, 1989, Collection of Mendocino County Museum, Acc.#89-28-1

5. Ibid.

6. Interview with Linda Aguilar McGill by David Ludwig, in Beverly R. Ortiz, *Pomo Basketweavers, A Tribute to Three Elders*, script pages 23-24, 1992

7. Interview with Susan Billy by Sandra Metzler with Dot Brovarney, August 5, 1989, Collection of Mendocino County Museum, Acc.#89-26-1

8. Ibid.

9. Susan Billy to Dot Brovarney, personal communication, 1993

10. Dugan Aguilar to Valerie Verzuh, personal communication, 1996

11. Aguilar to Metzler, Collection of Mendocino County Museum, Acc.#88-9-1

The Elsie Allen Collection

The following descriptions are based on these sources: Elsie Allen, Genevieve Allen Aguilar, Marion Steinbach, John Pryor, Susan Billy, Judith Polanich, and Foley Benson. In cases where conflicting information exists, identifications are based on the evaluation of composite data. Basket descriptions reflect notes and comments by Elsie Allen where possible. While many baskets serve multiple functions, the use specified by Mrs. Allen takes precedence in our descriptions.

Baskets #17, 79, 94, 118, and 140 are not currently part of the collection. Objects #11, 12, 137, 142, 143, and 144 are materials associated with basketry.

Photographs by Foley Benson.

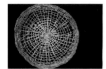

Elsie Allen
Work Basket, twined, open, plain (23.5 cm.)
Ukiah, Mendocino County, n.d.
Warp: unpeeled willow shoots
Weft: unpeeled willow shoots
Collection of Mendocino County Museum
Gift of Genevieve Allen Aguilar #89-33-1 (EA#1)

Elsie Allen
Work Basket, twined, plain (25.5 cm.)
Ukiah, Mendocino County, n.d.
Warp: unpeeled willow shoots
Weft: unpeeled willow shoots
Collection of Mendocino County Museum
Gift of Genevieve Allen Aguilar #89-33-2 (EA#2)

attributed to Annie Burke
Work Basket, twined, plain (40.5 cm.)
Hopland, Mendocino County, n.d.
Warp: unpeeled willow shoots
Weft: unpeeled willow shoots
Collection of Mendocino County Museum
Gift of Genevieve Allen Aguilar #89-33-3 (EA#3)

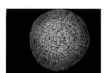

Annie Burke
Work Basket, twined, plain (56.5 cm)
Hopland, Mendocino County, n.d.
Warp: unpeeled willow shoots
Weft: unpeeled willow shoots
Collection of Mendocino County Museum
Gift of Genevieve Allen Aguilar #89-33-4 (EA#4)

unidentified weaver, n.d.
Work Basket, twined, open, plain (45.5 cm.)
Warp: unpeeled willow shoots
Weft: unpeeled willow shoots
Collection of Mendocino County Museum
Gift of Genevieve Allen Aguilar #89-33-5 (EA#5)

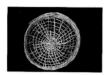

Annie Burke
Work Basket, twined, plain (52 cm.)
Hopland, Mendocino County, n.d.
Warp: peeled willow shoots
Weft: peeled and unpeeled willow shoots
Collection of Mendocino County Museum
Gift of Genevieve Allen Aguilar #89-33-6 (EA#6)

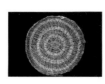

Non-Pomo (Asian or Pacific Islands), n.d.
Collection of Mendocino County Museum
Gift of Genevieve Allen Aguilar #89-33-7 (EA#7)

unidentified weaver, n.d.
Work Basket, twined, plain and lattice (50.5 cm.)
Warp: peeled willow shoots
Weft: prepared sedge roots with redbud
Collection of Mendocino County Museum
Gift of Genevieve Allen Aguilar #89-33-8 (EA#8)

unidentified weaver, n.d.
Work Basket, twined, plain (64 cm.)
Warp: unpeeled willow shoots
Weft: unpeeled willow shoots
Collection of Mendocino County Museum
Gift of Genevieve Allen Aguilar #89-33-9
(EA#9)

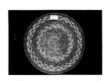

Annie Burke
Work Basket, twined, plain (66.5 cm)
Hopland, Mendocino County, n.d.
Warp: peeled willow shoots
Weft: peeled and unpeeled willow shoots
Collection of Genevieve Allen Aguilar (EA#10)

Elsie Allen
Baby Basket, model (13 cm.)
Ukiah, Mendocino County, n.d.
Materials: peeled willow sticks, oak (rim); cotton
string
Collection of Genevieve Allen Aguilar (EA#13)

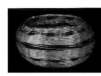

Annie Burke
Work Basket, twined, three strand (18 cm.)
Hopland, Mendocino County, c.1938
Warp: peeled willow shoots
Weft: peeled and unpeeled willow shoots
Collection of Genevieve Allen Aguilar (EA#22)

Elsie Allen
Baby Basket, model with doll (16 cm.)
Ukiah, Mendocino County, n.d.
Materials: peeled willow sticks, oak (rim); cotton
string
Collection of Genevieve Allen Aguilar (EA#14/15)

Mollie Jackson
Work Basket, twined, three strand (36 cm.)
Pinoleville Rancheria, Mendocino County, c.1960s
Warp: peeled whole willow shoots
Weft: peeled and unpeeled willow shoots
Collection of Mendocino County Museum
Gift of Genevieve Allen Aguilar #89-33-12 (EA#23)

Elsie Allen
Baby Basket, model (26.5 cm.)
Ukiah, Mendocino County, n.d.
Materials: peeled dogwood sticks, oak (rim);
cotton string
Collection of Genevieve Allen Aguilar (EA#16)

Annie Burke
Storage Basket, twined, open, lattice (40 cm.)
Hopland, Mendocino County, n.d.
Warp: peeled willow shoots
Weft: prepared sedge roots with redbud
Collection of Genevieve Allen Aguilar (EA#24)

unidentified weaver, n.d.
Baby Basket, model (24.5 cm.)
Materials: peeled dogwood or willow sticks, oak
(rim); cotton string, leather
Collection of Genevieve Allen Aguilar (EA#18)

Elsie Allen
Miniature Work Basket, twined, open, plain
(14 cm.)
Ukiah, Mendocino County, n.d.
Warp: peeled willow shoots
Weft: peeled willow shoots
Collection of Mendocino County Museum
Gift of Genevieve Allen Aguilar #89-33-13 (EA#25)

Elsie Allen
Baby Basket (40 cm.)
Ukiah, Mendocino County, n.d.
Materials: peeled dogwood sticks, oak (rim);
cotton string
Collection of Genevieve Allen Aguilar (EA#19)

Margaret McClure
Miniature Work Basket, twined, plain (10 cm.)
Ukiah, Mendocino County, n.d.
Warp: unpeeled willow shoots
Weft: unpeeled willow shoots
Collection of Mendocino County Museum
Gift of Genevieve Allen Aguilar #89-33-14
(EA#26)

Susan Billy recently identified Margaret McClure
as the weaver of basket EA#26. Mrs. McClure
was a student of Elsie Allen and, to date, is the
only non-Indian whose weaving is identified in
the Elsie Allen Collection.

Frank Miller's aunt
Pepperwood Nut Basket, twined, open, plain
(34.5 cm.)
Ukiah, Mendocino County, c.1900
Warp: peeled willow shoots
Weft: peeled willow shoots
Collection of Mendocino County Museum
Gift of Genevieve Allen Aguilar #89-33-10 (EA#20)

attributed to Mollie Jackson
Clover Serving Basket, twined, plain (33 cm.)
Pinoleville Rancheria, Mendocino County, n.d.
Warp: peeled willow shoots
Weft: peeled willow shoots
Collection of Mendocino County Museum
Gift of Genevieve Allen Aguilar #89-33-11
(EA#21)

unidentified weaver, n.d.
Work Basket, twined, plain and lattice (20 cm.)
Warp: peeled willow shoots
Weft: prepared sedge roots with redbud
Collection of Mendocino County Museum
Gift of Genevieve Allen Aguilar #89-33-15
(EA#27)

Annie Burke
Work Basket, twined, open, lattice (38 cm.)
Hopland, Mendocino County, n.d.
Warp: peeled willow shoots
Weft: prepared sedge roots with redbud
Collection of Genevieve Allen Aguilar (EA#28)

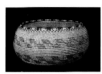

Annie Burke
Serving Basket, twined, open, lattice (31 cm.)
Hopland, Mendocino County, n.d.
Warp: peeled willow shoots
Weft: prepared sedge roots with redbud
Collection of Genevieve Allen Aguilar (EA#29)

Annie Burke
Serving Basket, twined, open, lattice (37 cm.)
Hopland, Mendocino County, c.1930
Warp: peeled willow shoots
Weft: prepared sedge roots with redbud
Collection of Genevieve Allen Aguilar (EA#30)

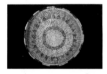

Annie Burke
Serving Basket, twined, plain, open, lattice
(26 cm.)
Hopland, Mendocino County, 1950
Warp: peeled willow shoots
Weft: prepared sedge roots with redbud
Collection of Genevieve Allen Aguilar (EA#31)

Maude Donohue Scott
Model Mortar Hopper, twined, plain and lattice
(26 cm.)
Yokayo Rancheria, Mendocino County, n.d.
Warp: peeled willow shoots
Weft: prepared sedge roots with redbud
Collection of Genevieve Allen Aguilar (EA#32)

Agnes Santana's grandmother (Mrs. Kyman)
Mortar Hopper, twined, plain and lattice
(38.5 cm.)
Warp: peeled willow shoots
Weft: prepared sedge roots with redbud
Collection of Genevieve Allen Aguilar (EA#33)

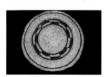

unidentified weaver, n.d.
Work Basket, twined, plain and lattice (38 cm.)
Warp: peeled willow shoots
Weft: prepared sedge roots with redbud
Collection of Genevieve Allen Aguilar (EA#34)

unidentified weaver, n.d.
Storage Basket, twined, plain (23 cm.)
Warp: peeled willow shoots
Weft: peeled willow shoots with redbud
Collection of Mendocino County Museum
Gift of Genevieve Allen Aguilar #89-33-16
(EA#35)

Mollie Jackson
Work Basket, twined, three strand (28.5 cm.)
Pinoleville Rancheria, Mendocino County,
c.1930
Warp: peeled willow shoots
Weft: peeled and unpeeled willow shoots
Collection of Genevieve Allen Aguilar (EA#36)

attributed to Laura Wilbell
Serving Basket, twined, three strand (37 cm.)
Hopland Rancheria, Mendocino County, n.d.
Warp: peeled willow shoots
Weft: peeled willow shoots
Collection of Mendocino County Museum
Gift of Genevieve Allen Aguilar #89-33-17
(EA#37)

Mow-sha Wilbell Edwards
Storage Basket, twined, plain (21 cm.)
Hopland, Mendocino County, 1908
Warp: peeled willow shoots
Weft: peeled willow shoots
Collection of Mendocino County Museum
Gift of Genevieve Allen Aguilar #89-33-18
(EA#38)

unidentified weaver, n.d.
Work Basket, twined, lattice (23 cm.)
Warp: peeled willow shoots
Weft: prepared sedge roots with redbud
Collection of Mendocino County Museum
Gift of Genevieve Allen Aguilar #89-33-19
(EA#39)

unidentified weaver, n.d.
Work Basket, twined, diagonal (25 cm.)
Warp: peeled willow shoots
Weft: prepared sedge roots with redbud
Collection of Mendocino County Museum
Gift of Genevieve Allen Aguilar #89-33-20
(EA#40)

Annie Burke
Storage Basket, twined, lattice (29 cm.)
Hopland, Mendocino County, c.1930
Warp: peeled willow shoots
Weft: prepared sedge roots with redbud
Collection of Genevieve Allen Aguilar (EA#41)

Maude Donohue Scott or Annie Burke
Cooking Basket, twined, lattice (42 cm.)
Yokayo Rancheria or Hopland Rancheria,
Mendocino County, n.d.
Warp: peeled willow shoots
Weft: prepared sedge roots with redbud
Collection of Genevieve Allen Aguilar (EA#42)

Salome Alcantra
Canoe Basket, coiled (55 x 35 cm.)
Yokayo Rancheria, Mendocino County, 1978
Foundation: 1-rod, scraped willow shoots
Weaving Element: prepared sedge roots with
split redbud
Collection of Genevieve Allen Aguilar (EA#49)

unidentified weaver, n.d.
Burden Basket, twined, plain, diagonal (46 cm.)
Warp: peeled willow shoots
Weft: prepared sedge roots with redbud
Collection of Genevieve Allen Aguilar (EA#43)

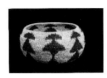

Salome Alcantra
Basket, bowl, coiled (18 cm.)
Yokayo Rancheria, Mendocino County, 1982
Foundation: 1-rod, scraped willow shoots
Weaving Element: prepared sedge roots with
redbud
Collection of Mendocino County Museum
Gift of Genevieve Allen Aguilar #89-33-21 (EA#50)

unidentified weaver, pre-1884
Burden Basket, twined, diagonal (46 cm.)
Warp: peeled willow shoots
Weft: prepared sedge roots with redbud
Collection of Genevieve Allen Aguilar (EA#44)

Rhoda Knight
Basket, coiled (19 cm.)
Yokayo Rancheria, Mendocino County,
c.1930s
Foundation: 3-rod, scraped willow shoots
Weaving Element: prepared sedge roots with
bulrush
Collection of Genevieve Allen Aguilar (EA#51)

Annie Burke
Miniature Burden Basket, twined, plain (14 cm.)
Hopland, Mendocino County, n.d.
Warp: peeled willow shoots
Weft: prepared sedge roots with redbud
Collection of Genevieve Allen Aguilar (EA#45)

unidentified weaver (non-Pomo), n.d.
Patwin Basket, coiled (17 cm.)
Collection of Genevieve Allen Aguilar (EA#52)

Annie Burke
Miniature Burden Basket, twined, plain (8.5 cm.)
Hopland, Mendocino County, n.d.
Warp: peeled willow shoots
Weft: prepared sedge roots with redbud
Collection of Genevieve Allen Aguilar (EA#46)

Alice Elliott
Basket, coiled (13 cm.)
Hopland, Mendocino County, n.d.
Foundation: 1-rod, scraped willow shoots
Weaving Element: prepared sedge roots with
redbud
Collection of Genevieve Allen Aguilar (EA#53)

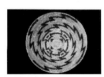

Annie Lake
Serving Basket, coiled (32 cm.)
Redwood Valley, Mendocino County, c.1945
Foundation: 1-rod, scraped willow shoots
Weaving Element: prepared sedge roots with
redbud
Collection of Genevieve Allen Aguilar (EA#47)

Elsie Allen
Basket, coiled (11 cm.)
Ukiah, Mendocino County, c.1979
Foundation: 1-rod, scraped willow shoots
Weaving Element: prepared sedge roots with
bulrush
Collection of Genevieve Aguilar (EA#54)

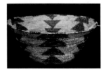

unidentified weaver, n.d.
Basket, flared, coiled (40.5 cm.)
Foundation: 1-rod, scraped willow shoots
Weaving Element: prepared sedge roots with
redbud
Collection of Genevieve Allen Aguilar (EA#48)

Nora Cooper
Basket, coiled (9.5 cm.)
Guidiville Rancheria, Mendocino County, n.d.
Foundation: 1-rod, scraped willow shoots
Weaving Element: prepared sedge roots with
bulrush
Collection of Genevieve Allen Aguilar (EA#55)

Alice Elliott
Basket, coiled (9 cm.)
Hopland, Mendocino County, 1944 or 1972
Foundation: 1-rod, scraped willow shoots
Weaving Element: prepared sedge roots with
bulrush
Collection of Genevieve Allen Aguilar (EA#56)

Myrtle McKay Chavez
Canoe Basket, coiled (19 cm.)
Windsor, Sonoma County, n.d.
Foundation: 3-rod, scraped shoots
Weaving Element: prepared sedge roots with
bulrush
Collection of Genevieve Allen Aguilar (EA#57)

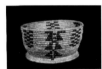

unidentified weaver, n.d.
Basket, coiled (20 cm.)
Foundation: 3-rod, scraped willow shoots
Weaving Element: prepared sedge roots with
bulrush
Collection of Mendocino County Museum
Gift of Genevieve Allen Aguilar #89-33-22
(EA#58)

unidentified weaver (non-Pomo), n.d.
Sierra Miwok or Maidu Basket, coiled (21 cm.)
Collection of Mendocino County Museum
Gift of Genevieve Allen Aguilar #89-33-23
(EA#59)

**attributed to Agnes Santana's grandmother
(Mrs. Kyman)**
Basket, lattice twined with coiled foot (19 cm.)
Warp: peeled willow shoots
Weft: prepared sedge roots with redbud
Collection of Genevieve Allen Aguilar (EA#60)

Annie Lake
Gift Basket, beaded, coiled (12 cm.)
Redwood Valley, Mendocino County, 1984
Foundation: 1-rod, scraped willow shoots
Weaving Element: prepared sedge roots with red,
green glass beads
Collection of Genevieve Allen Aguilar (EA#61)

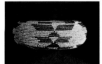

Annie Lake
Canoe Gift Basket, beaded, coiled (15 x 18 cm.)
Redwood Valley, Mendocino County, n.d.
Foundation: 1-rod, scraped willow shoots
Weaving Element: prepared sedge roots with red,
white, black, blue glass beads
Collection of Genevieve Allen Aguilar (EA#62)

Lydia Faught
Gift Basket, beaded, coiled (27 cm.)
Upper Lake Rancheria, Lake County, c.1920–25
Foundation: 1-rod, scraped willow shoots
Weaving Element: prepared sedge roots with
black, blue, white, clear, brown, green, red,
lavender, baby blue glass beads
Collection of Genevieve Allen Aguilar (EA#63)

Mary Arnold
Gift Basket, beaded, coiled (16 cm.)
Cloverdale, Sonoma County, 1916
Foundation: 1-rod, scraped willow shoots
Weaving Element: prepared sedge roots with
redbud and black, yellow, white glass beads
Collection of Genevieve Allen Aguilar (EA#64)

Annie Lake
Gift Basket, beaded, coiled (14 cm.)
Redwood Valley, Mendocino County, n.d.
Foundation: 1-rod, scraped willow shoots
Weaving Element: prepared sedge roots with
cobalt blue, yellow glass beads
Collection of Genevieve Allen Aguilar (EA#65)

Annie Lake
Canoe Gift Basket, beaded, coiled (12 cm.)
Redwood Valley, Mendocino County, n.d.
Foundation: 1-rod, scraped willow shoots
Weaving Element: prepared sedge roots with
blue, white glass beads
Collection of Genevieve Allen Aguilar (EA#66)

Annie Lake
Gift Basket, beaded, coiled (10 cm.)
Redwood Valley, Mendocino County, n.d.
Foundation: 1-rod, scraped willow shoots
Weaving Element: prepared sedge roots with red,
blue glass beads
Collection of Genevieve Allen Aguilar (EA#67)

Annie Lake
Gift Basket, beaded, coiled (11 cm.)
Redwood Valley, Mendocino County, n.d.
Foundation: 1-rod, scraped willow shoots
Weaving Element: prepared sedge roots with
blue, green, orange glass beads.
Collection of Genevieve Allen Aguilar (EA#68)

Annie Lake
Canoe Gift Basket, beaded, coiled (6 cm.)
Redwood Valley, Mendocino County, n.d.
Foundation: 1-rod, scraped willow shoots
Weaving Element: prepared sedge roots with
yellow, red glass beads
Collection of Genevieve Allen Aguilar (EA#69)

unidentified weaver, n.d.
Gift Basket, beaded, coiled (12 cm.)
Foundation: 1-rod, scraped willow shoots
Weaving Element: prepared sedge roots with
yellow, blue, black, orange glass beads
Collection of Genevieve Allen Aguilar (EA#70)

Elsie Allen
Miniature Gift Basket, beaded, coiled (5 cm.)
Ukiah, Mendocino County, 1976
Foundation: 1-rod, scraped willow shoots
Weaving Element: prepared sedge roots with
white, blue glass beads
Collection of Genevieve Allen Aguilar (EA#71)

Elsie Allen
Gift Basket, beaded, coiled (9 cm.)
Ukiah, Mendocino County, n.d.
Foundation: 1-rod, scraped willow shoots
Weaving Element: prepared sedge roots with
yellow, blue glass beads; quail topknots
Collection of Genevieve Allen Aguilar (EA#72)

unidentified weaver, n.d.
Canoe Gift Basket, coiled (26 cm.)
Foundation: 1-rod, scraped willow shoots
Weaving Element: prepared sedge roots with
bulrush, quail topknot feathers
Collection of Genevieve Allen Aguilar (EA#73)

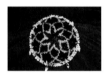

Suzanne Holder
Gift Basket, feathered, coiled (20 cm.)
Upper Lake Rancheria, Lake County, n.d.
Foundation: 3-rod, scraped willow shoots
Weaving Element: prepared sedge roots with
mallard duck, meadowlark, oriole, quail
topknots, clamshell disk beads, abalone pendants
Collection of Genevieve Allen Aguilar (EA#74)

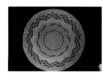

Annie Burke
Work Basket, twined, plain and lattice (55.5 cm.)
Hopland, Mendocino County, c.1925
Warp: peeled willow shoots
Weft: prepared sedge roots with redbud
Collection of Genevieve Allen Aguilar (EA#75)

Annie Boone
Gift Basket, feathered, coiled (19 cm.)
Upper Lake Rancheria, Lake County, n.d.
Foundation: 3-rod, scraped willow shoots
Weaving Element: prepared sedge roots with
mallard duck, meadowlark, quail topknots,
oriole, clamshell disk beads
Collection of Genevieve Allen Aguilar (EA#76)

Suzanne Holder
Gift Basket, feathered, coiled (17 cm.)
Upper Lake Rancheria, Lake County, n.d.
Foundation: 3-rod, scraped willow shoots
Weaving Element: prepared sedge roots with
mallard, meadowlark, quail topknots, oriole, clam-
shell disk beads and pendants, abalone pendants
Collection of Genevieve Allen Aguilar (EA#77)

Elsie Allen
Gift Basket, feathered, coiled (14 cm.)
Ukiah, Mendocino County, 1976
Foundation: 3-rod, scraped willow shoots
Weaving Element: prepared sedge roots with
mallard duck, meadowlark, quail topknots
Collection of Genevieve Allen Aguilar (EA#78)

Elsie Allen
Gift Basket, feathered, coiled (11 cm.)
Ukiah, Mendocino County, 1977
Foundation: 3-rod, scraped willow shoots
Weaving Element: prepared sedge roots with quail
topknots, pheasant, clamshell disk beads
Collection of Genevieve Allen Aguilar (EA#80)

Annie Lake
Gift Basket, feathered, coiled (11 cm.)
Redwood Valley, Mendocino County, 1975
Foundation: 3-rod, scraped willow shoots
Weaving Element: prepared sedge roots with
bulrush, woodpecker
Collection of Genevieve Allen Aguilar (EA#81)

Elsie Allen
Gift Basket, feathered, coiled (9 cm.)
Ukiah, Mendocino County, 1975
Foundation: 3-rod, scraped willow shoots
Weaving Element: prepared sedge roots with quail
topknots, pheasant
Collection of Genevieve Allen Aguilar (EA#82)

unidentified weaver, n.d.
Miniature Gift Basket, feathered, coiled (8 cm.)
Foundation: 3-rod, cane?
Weaving Element: prepared sedge roots with
pheasant feathers
Collection of Genevieve Allen Aguilar (EA#83)

Annie Lake
Miniature Gift Basket, feathered, coiled (5.4 cm.)
Redwood Valley, Mendocino County, 1971
Foundation: 1-rod, scraped willow shoots
Weaving Element: prepared sedge roots with
mallard duck, white glass beads
Collection of Genevieve Allen Aguilar (EA#84)

Annie Lake
Miniature Gift Basket, feathered, coiled (5 cm.)
Foundation: 3-rod, scraped willow shoots
Weaving Element: prepared sedge roots with
mallard duck, meadowlark
Collection of Genevieve Allen Aguilar (EA#85)

unidentified weaver, n.d.
Miniature Canoe Basket, coiled (4.5 cm.)
Foundation: 1-rod, unsplit sedge
Weaving Element: prepared sedge roots with
bulrush
Collection of Genevieve Allen Aguilar (EA#92)

Annie Lake
Miniature Gift Basket, feathered, coiled (2.2 cm.)
Redwood Valley, Mendocino County, 1972
Foundation: sedge bundle
Weaving Element: prepared sedge roots with
mallard duck, oriole
Collection of Genevieve Allen Aguilar (EA#86)

unidentified weaver, n.d.
Miniature Canoe Basket, coiled (3.5 cm.)
Foundation: 1-rod, probably unsplit sedge or
bulrush
Weaving Element: prepared sedge roots with
bulrush
Collection of Genevieve Allen Aguilar (EA#93)

Evelyn Lake
Miniature Basket, coiled (2.4 cm.)
Redwood Valley, Mendocino County, 1943–44
Foundation: 1-rod, scraped willow shoots
Weaving Element: prepared sedge roots with
bulrush
Collection of Genevieve Allen Aguilar (EA#87)

unidentified weaver, n.d.
Fish Trap Basket, twined, open, plain (42.5 cm.)
Warp: unpeeled willow shoots
Weft: unpeeled willow shoots
Collection of Genevieve Allen Aguilar (EA#95)

Mollie Jackson
Miniature Basket, coiled (5 cm.)
Pinoleville Rancheria, Mendocino County,
c.1972
Foundation: 1-rod, scraped willow shoots
Weaving Element: prepared sedge roots with
bulrush
Collection of Genevieve Allen Aguilar (EA#88)

unidentified weaver, n.d.
Miniature Baby Basket (2.7 cm.)
Materials: peeled willow sticks, cotton string
Collection of Genevieve Allen Aguilar (EA#96)

Laura Somersal
Miniature Basket, coiled (4.7 cm.)
Dry Creek Rancheria, Sonoma County, n.d.
Foundation: sedge bundle
Weaving Element: prepared sedge roots with
bulrush
Collection of Genevieve Allen Aguilar (EA#89)

unidentified weaver, n.d.
Miniature Baby Basket (7 cm.)
Materials: peeled willow sticks, cotton string
Collection of Genevieve Allen Aguilar (EA#97)

Laura Somersal
Miniature Basket, coiled (3.8 cm.)
Dry Creek Rancheria, Sonoma County, n.d.
Foundation: sedge bundle
Weaving Element: prepared sedge roots with
bulrush
Collection of Genevieve Allen Aguilar (EA#90)

unidentified weaver, n.d.
Miniature Baby Baskct (8 cm.)
Materials: peeled willow sticks, cotton string
Collection of Genevieve Allen Aguilar (EA#98)

unidentified weaver, n.d.
Miniature Basket, coiled (1.9 cm.)
Foundation: 1-rod, unsplit sedge
Weaving Element: prepared sedge roots with
bulrush
Collection of Genevieve Allen Aguilar (EA#91)

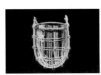

unidentified weaver, n.d.
Miniature Baby Basket (8 cm.)
Materials: peeled willow sticks, cotton string
Collection of Genevieve Allen Aguilar (EA#99)

Laura Somersal
Miniature Basket, coiled (4 cm.)
Dry Creek Rancheria, Sonoma County, n.d.
Foundation: sedge bundle
Weaving Element: prepared sedge roots with bulrush
Collection of Genevieve Allen Aguilar (EA#100)

Laura Somersal
Miniature Canoe Basket, coiled (1.3 x 2.1 cm.)
Dry Creek Rancheria, Sonoma County, c.1980
Foundation: 1-rod, scraped willow shoots
Weaving Element: prepared sedge roots with bulrush
Collection of Genevieve Allen Aguilar (EA#107)

Laura Somersal
Miniature Basket, coiled (2.5 cm.)
Dry Creek Rancheria, Sonoma County, n.d.
Foundation: sedge bundle
Weaving Element: prepared sedge roots with bulrush
Collection of Genevieve Allen Aguilar (EA#101)

Elsie Allen
Miniature Basket, coiled (3.5 cm.)
Ukiah, Mendocino County, 1979
Foundation: 1-rod, scraped willow shoots
Weaving Element: prepared sedge roots with bulrush
Collection of Genevieve Allen Aguilar (EA#108)

Laura Somersal
Miniature Basket, coiled (1.9 cm.)
Dry Creek Rancheria, Sonoma County, n.d.
Foundation: sedge bundle
Weaving Element: prepared sedge roots with bulrush
Collection of Genevieve Allen Aguilar (EA#102)

Elsie Allen
Miniature Basket, coiled (3.1 cm.)
Ukiah, Mendocino County, 1978
Foundation: 1-rod, scraped willow shoots
Weaving Element: prepared sedge roots with bulrush
Collection of Genevieve Allen Aguilar (EA#109)

Laura Somersal
Miniature Basket, coiled (1.8 cm.)
Dry Creek Rancheria, Sonoma County, n.d.
Foundation: sedge bundle
Weaving Element: prepared sedge roots with bulrush
Collection of Genevieve Allen Aguilar (EA#103)

Elsie Allen
Miniature Basket, coiled (1.9 cm.)
Ukiah, Mendocino County, n.d.
Foundation: 1-rod, probably unsplit sedge or bulrush
Weaving Element: prepared sedge roots with bulrush
Collection of Genevieve Allen Aguilar (EA#110)

Laura Somersal
Miniature Basket, coiled (1.5 cm.)
Dry Creek Rancheria, Sonoma County, n.d.
Foundation: sedge bundle
Weaving Element: prepared sedge roots with bulrush
Collection of Genevieve Allen Aguilar (EA#104)

Elsie Allen
Miniature Basket, coiled (1.75 cm.)
Ukiah, Mendocino County, 1972
Foundation: 1-rod, probably unsplit sedge or bulrush
Weaving Element: prepared sedge roots with bulrush
Collection of Genevieve Allen Aguilar (EA#111)

Laura Somersal
Miniature Basket, coiled (0.9 cm.)
Dry Creek Rancheria, Sonoma County, n.d.
Foundation: sedge bundle
Weaving Element: prepared sedge roots with bulrush
Collection of Genevieve Allen Aguilar (EA#105)

Elsie Allen
Miniature Basket, coiled (1.7 cm.)
Ukiah, Mendocino County, 1972
Foundation: 1-rod, probably unsplit sedge or bulrush
Weaving Element: prepared sedge roots with bulrush
Collection of Genevieve Allen Aguilar (EA#112)

Laura Somersal
Miniature Basket, coiled (1.4 cm.)
Dry Creek Rancheria, Sonoma County, n.d.
Foundation: sedge bundle
Weaving Element: prepared sedge roots with bulrush
Collection of Genevieve Allen Aguilar (EA#106)

Elsie Allen
Miniature Basket, coiled (.8 cm.)
Ukiah, Mendocino County, n.d.
Foundation: 1-rod, probably unsplit sedge or bulrush
Weaving Element: prepared sedge roots with bulrush
Collection of Genevieve Allen Aguilar (EA#113)

Elsie Allen
Jewelry Disk, coiled (5.5 cm.)
Ukiah, Mendocino County, n.d.
Foundation: 1-rod, scraped willow shoots
Weaving Element: prepared sedge roots with
redbud
Collection of Genevieve Allen Aguilar (EA#114)

Susan Billy
Miniature Gift Basket, coiled (.7 cm.)
Ukiah, Mendocino County, c.1975
Foundation: 1-rod, unsplit sedge
Weaving Element: prepared sedge roots
Collection of Genevieve Allen Aguilar (EA#122)

Elsie Allen
Jewelry Disk, coiled (6 cm.)
Ukiah, Mendocino County, n.d.
Foundation: 1-rod, scraped willow shoots
Weaving Element: prepared sedge roots with
redbud
Collection of Genevieve Allen Aguilar (EA#115)

unidentified weaver, n.d.
Miniature Canoe Basket, coiled (.3 x .5 cm.)
Foundation: 1-rod, probably unsplit sedge or
bulrush
Weaving Element: prepared sedge roots with
bulrush
Collection of Genevieve Allen Aguilar (EA#123)

Elsie Allen
Jewelry Disk, coiled (6.2 cm.)
Ukiah, Mendocino County, n.d.
Foundation: 1-rod, scraped willow shoots
Weaving Element: prepared sedge roots with
bulrush
Collection of Genevieve Allen Aguilar (EA#116)

unidentified weaver, n.d.
Miniature Canoe Basket, coiled (.7 cm.)
Foundation: 1-rod, probably unsplit sedge or
bulrush
Weaving Element: prepared sedge roots with
bulrush
Collection of Genevieve Allen Aguilar (EA#124)

Elsie Allen
Jewelry Disk, coiled (7.8 cm.)
Ukiah, Mendocino County, n.d.
Foundation: 1-rod, scraped willow shoots
Weaving Element: prepared sedge roots with
redbud
Collection of Genevieve Allen Aguilar (EA#117)

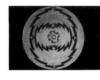

Salome Alcantra
Basket Tray, coiled (45.5 cm.)
Yokayo Rancheria, Mendocino County, n.d.
Foundation: 1-rod, scraped willow shoots
Weaving Element: prepared sedge roots with
bulrush
Collection of Genevieve Allen Aguilar (EA#125)

Gladys Lockhart
Miniature Basket, coiled (0.6 cm.)
Pinoleville Rancheria, Mendocino County, n.d.
Foundation: 1-rod, probably unsplit sedge
Weaving Element: prepared sedge roots with
bulrush
Collection of Genevieve Allen Aguilar (EA#119)

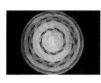

unidentified weaver, n.d.
Work Basket, twined, plain, lattice (41.5 cm.)
Warp: peeled willow shoots
Weft: prepared sedge roots with redbud
Collection of Genevieve Allen Aguilar (EA#126)

Gladys Lockhart
Miniature Basket, coiled (0.5 cm.)
Pinoleville Rancheria, Mendocino County, n.d.
Foundation: 1-rod, probably unsplit sedge
Weaving Element: prepared sedge roots with
bulrush
Collection of Genevieve Allen Aguilar (EA#120)

Maude Donohue Scott
Cooking Basket, twined, diagonal (20 cm.)
Yokayo Rancheria, Mendocino County, n.d.
Warp: peeled willow shoots
Weft: prepared sedge roots with redbud
Collection of Genevieve Allen Aguilar (EA#127)

Gladys Lockhart
Miniature Basket, coiled (0.5 cm.)
Pinoleville Rancheria, Mendocino County, n.d.
Foundation: 1-rod, probably unsplit sedge
Weaving Element: prepared sedge roots with
bulrush
Collection of Genevieve Allen Aguilar (EA#121)

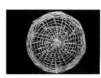

unidentified weaver, n.d.
Work Basket, twined, open, plain (28 cm.)
Warp: unpeeled willow shoots
Weft: unpeeled willow shoots
Collection of Mendocino County Museum
Gift of Genevieve Allen Aguilar 89-33-24
(EA#128)

Annie Burke
Cooking Basket, twined, plain (22 cm.)
Hopland, Mendocino County, n.d.
Warp: peeled willow shoots
Weft: split sedge roots with redbud
Collection of Genevieve Allen Aguilar (EA#129)

Susie Santiago Billy
Gift Basket, feathered, coiled (20.8 cm.)
Hopland, Mendocino County, n.d.
Foundation: 3-rod, scraped willow shoots
Weaving Element: prepared sedge roots with
mallard duck, meadowlark, quail topknots,
clamshell disk beads, abalone pendants
Collection of Genevieve Allen Aguilar (EA#130)

Wala Wala
Ceremonial Basket, coiled (26 cm.)
Hopland, Mendocino County, n.d.
Foundation: 1-rod, scraped willow shoots
Weaving Element: prepared sedge roots with
bulrush, clamshell disk beads, abalone pendants,
cotton string.
Collection of Genevieve Allen Aguilar (EA#131)

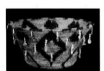

Annie Burke
Canoe Basket, coiled (21 cm.)
Hopland, Mendocino County, c.1924
Foundation: 1-rod, scraped willow shoots
Weaving Element: prepared sedge roots with
bulrush
Collection of Genevieve Allen Aguilar (EA#132)

Annie Burke
Basket, coiled (17 cm.)
Hopland, Mendocino County, c.1930s
Foundation: 1-rod, scraped willow shoots
Weaving Element: prepared sedge roots with
bulrush
Collection of Genevieve Allen Aguilar (EA#133)

Annie Burke
Gift Basket, feathered, coiled (15 cm.)
Hopland, Mendocino County, 1940
Foundation: 3-rod, scraped willow shoots
Weaving Element: prepared sedge roots with
bulrush, woodpecker
Collection of Genevieve Allen Aguilar (EA#134)

Ethel Burke
Basket, coiled (16 cm.)
Hopland, Mendocino County, n.d.
Foundation: 1-rod, scraped willow shoots
Weaving Element: prepared sedge roots with
bulrush
Collection of Genevieve Allen Aguilar (EA#135)

Agnes Santana
Basket, coiled (15 cm.)
Cloverdale Rancheria, Sonoma County, n.d.
Foundation: 1-rod, scraped willow shoots
Weaving Element: prepared sedge roots with
bulrush
Collection of Genevieve Allen Aguilar (EA#136)

Annie Burke
Basketry Placemat, coiled (27 cm.)
Hopland, Mendocino County, 1942
Foundation: 1-rod, scraped willow shoots
Weaving Element: prepared sedge roots with
bulrush
Collection of Genevieve Allen Aguilar (EA#138)

Annie Burke
Basketry Placemat, coiled (27.5 cm.)
Hopland, Mendocino County, 1942
Foundation: 1-rod, scraped willow shoots
Weaving Element: prepared sedge roots with
bulrush
Collection of Genevieve Allen Aguilar (EA#139)

Elsie Allen
Baby Basket, model, unfinished (47 cm.)
Ukiah, Mendocino County, c.1980
Materials: peeled willow sticks, white cotton
string
Collection of Genevieve Allen Aguilar (EA#141)

Baskets, page 42 and page 105:

Laura Wilbell (47 cm.)
Burden Basket, twined, open, plain
Warp: peeled willow shoots
Weft: peeled willow shoots
Private Collection

Susan Billy
Basket, coiled (11.5 cm.)
Foundation: 1-rod, scraped willow shoots
Weaving Element: prepared sedge roots with redbud, bauxite beads
Private Collection

Susan Billy
Miniature Gift Basket, feathered, coiled (6 cm.)
Foundation: 1-rod, scraped willow shoots
Weaving Element: prepared sedge roots with pheasant feathers
Private Collection

Key to Common Names

willow-*Salix* spp.	mallard -*Ana platyrhynchos*
sedge-*Carex* spp.	oriole-*Icterus galbula*
redbud-*Cercis occidentalis*	meadowlark-*Sturnella neglecta*
bulrush-*Scirpus* spp.	pheasant-*Phasianus colchicus*
creek dogwood-*Cornus glabrata*	clamshell-*Saxidomus nuttallii*
California quail-*Callipepla californica*	abalone-*Haliotis* spp.

Photograph Credits

Facing front cover: Private collection. The authors are indebted to Verle Anderson whose efforts through the Native American History Project in Ukiah led to identification of the majority of people in this photograph. Her consultants included Francis Maize, Bob Jackson, Edgar and Pearl Jackson, Esther Lockhart and Grace Williams Duncan. Susan Billy consulted with Elsie Allen, Ethel Burke, Matthew Billy, and Virginia Knight Buck in making a number of the identifications.

Facing title page: Collection of Genevieve Allen Aguilar

Color photographs of baskets by Catherine Buchanan

Photographs, index to the Elsie Allen Collection, by Foley Benson

Bibliography

Aginsky, B.W. and E.G.
1971   *Deep Valley*, New York, NY: Stein and Day.

Allen, Elsie
1972   *Pomo Basketmaking, A Supreme Art of the Weaver*, Happy Camp: Naturegraph Publishers.

Barrett, Samuel A.
1908   Pomo Indian Basketry. *University of California Publications in American Archaeology and Ethnology* 7(3):133-299. Reprinted in 1976 by The Rio Grande Press, Inc., Glorieta, NM.

Bates, Craig
1983   The Big Pomo Basket. *American Indian Basketry* 3(3):12-14.

Beard, Yolanda S.
1979   *The Wappo: A Report*, Banning, CA: Malki Museum Press.

Blackburn, Thomas C., and Kat Anderson
1993   *Before the Wilderness: Environmental Management by Native Californians*, Menlo Park, CA: Ballena Press.

Heizer, Robert F., ed.
1978   *Handbook of the North American Indians, v.8*, Washington, DC: Smithsonian Institution.

Hudson, J.W.
1893   Pomo Basket Makers. *Overland Monthly* 21:561-578. Second series.

Keator, Glenn, Linda Yamane, and Ann Lewis
1995   *In Full View: Three Ways of Seeing California Plants*, Berkeley: Heyday Books.

Kroeber, Alfred
1976   *Handbook of the Indians of California*, New York: Dover Publications, Inc.
1909   California Basketry and the Pomo. *American Anthropologist* II: 233-249.

Mason, Otis T.
1902   *Aboriginal American Basketry: Studies in a Textile Art Without Machinery*, Washington, D.C.: Smithsonian Institution, Annual Report, pp. 171-548. Reprinted in 1972 by Rio Grande Press, Inc., Glorieta, NM.

McLendon, Sally
1993   Collecting Pomoan Baskets, 1889-1939. *Museum Anthropology* 17(2):49-60.
1992   California Baskets and Basketmakers. *Basketmakers: Meaning and Form in Native American Baskets*, Linda Mowat, Howard Morphy, and Penny Dransart, eds. Oxford, England: University of Oxford. Pitt Rivers Museum Monograph 6, pp. 51-76.
1990   Pomo Baskets: The Legacy of William and Mary Benson. *Native Peoples* 4(1):26-33.
1981   Preparing Museum Collections for Use as Primary Data in Ethnographic Research. *The Research Potential of Anthropological Museum Collections*, Anne-Marie Cantwell, James B. Griffin, and Nan A. Rothschild, eds. New York, NY: Academy of Sciences, Annals of the New York Academy of Sciences 376, pp. 201-227.

McLendon, Sally, and Brenda Shears-Holland
1979   The Basketmakers: The Pomoans of California. *The Ancestors, Native Artists of the Americas*. A.C. Roosevelt and J.G.E. Smith, eds. New York, NY: Museum of the American Indian, pp. 103-129.

McLendon, Sally, and Robert Oswalt
1978   Pomo: An Introduction. *Handbook of North American Indians*, Volume 8, California, Robert F. Heizer, ed. Washington, D.C.: Smithsonian Institution.

Moser, Christopher L.
1989   *American Indian Basketry of Central California*, Riverside, CA: Riverside Museum Press.

Newman, Sandra Corrie
1974   *Indian Basket Weaving, How to Weave Pomo, Yurok, Pima and Navajo Baskets*, Flagstaff, AZ: Northland Press, pp. 3-22.

Nicholson, Grace
[n.d.]   List of Indian Baskets Made by Mary and William Benson-Pomo Tribe. New York, NY: Museum of the American Indian Archives.

Ortiz, Beverly R.
1993   Contemporary California Indian Basketweavers and the Environment. *Before the Wilderness: Environmental Management by Native Californians*, Thomas C. Blackburn and Kat Anderson, eds. Menlo Park, CA: Ballena Press, pp. 195-212.
1991/92   California Indian Basketweavers Gathering, A Special Report, Beverly R. Ortiz, ed. *News from Native California* 6(1):16-17.

Patterson, Scott M.
1989   *A Sense of Place, California North Coast Ethnographic Photography*, Ukiah and Willits, CA: Grace Hudson Museum and Mendocino County Museum.

Peri, David W., and Scott M. Patterson
1976   The Basket is in the Roots, That's Where it Begins. *Journal of California Anthropology* 3(2):17-32. Reprinted in *Before the Wilderness: Environmental Management by Native Californians*, Thomas C. Blackburn and Kat Anderson, eds., 1993 by Ballena Press, Menlo Park, CA.

Peri, David W., Scott M. Patterson, and Jennie Goodrich.
1985   *Ethnobotanical Mitigation, Warm Springs Dam—Lake Sonoma, California*. San Francisco, CA: U.S. Army Corps of Engineers

Peri, David W., Scott M. Patterson, and Susan L. McMurray
1985   *The Makahmo Pomo: An Ethnographic Survey of the Cloverdale (Makahmo) Pomo*. San Francisco, CA: United States Army Corps of Engineers.

Purdy, Carl
1901-02   The Pomo Indian Baskets and Their Makers. *Out West* XV(6):438-449, XVI(1):8-19, XVI(2):150-158, XVI(3):262-273. Reprinted by Mendocino County Historical Society, Ukiah, CA, n.d.

Roosevelt, Anna Curtenius and James G.E. Smith
1979   *The Ancestors, Native Artists of the Americas*, New York, NY: Museum of the American Indian.

Sarris, Greg
1995   *Mabel McKay: Weaving the Dream*, Berkeley, CA: University of California Press.

Smith-Ferri, Sherrie
1993   Basket Weavers, Basket Collectors, and the Market: A Case Study of Joseppa Dick. *Museum Anthropology* 17(2):61-66.
[1990]   Webs of Meaning: Pomoan Baskets, Their Creators and Their Collectors. Research Competency Paper, University of Washington, Seattle

Theodoratus, Dorothea J., David W. Peri, Clinton M. Blount, and Scott M. Patterson
1975   *An Ethnographic Survey of the Mahilkaune (Dry Creek) Pomo*. San Francisco, CA: United States Army Corps of Engineers.

Winther, Barbara
1985   Pomo Banded Baskets and Their Dau Marks. *American Indian Art* 10(4):50-57.

Remember Your Relations: The Elsie Allen Baskets, Family & Friends

Project Staff and Support

Suzanne Abel-Vidor, Exhibit Co-Curator, Grace Hudson Museum, City of Ukiah
Susan Billy, Guest Curator, Oakland and Hudson Museum presentations
Dot Brovarney, Exhibit Co-Curator, Grace Hudson Museum, City of Ukiah
Bette Fairbairn, Museum Assistant, Grace Hudson Museum
Keith White Wolf James, Technical Consultant, Grace Hudson Museum
Carey Caldwell, Senior Curator of History, Oakland Museum of California, Project Director
L. Thomas Frye, Chief Curator of History, Oakland Museum of California
Dennis M. Power, Executive Director, Oakland Museum of California
Lisette Reynolds, Curatorial Aide, Oakland Museum of California
Valerie Verzuh, Curatorial Assistant, Oakland Museum of California
Jeannine Gendar, Editor, Heyday Books
Wendy Low, Editorial Assistant, Heyday Books
Malcolm Margolin, Publisher, Heyday Books

Family Consultants

Lena Cordova Abasolo
Dugan Aguilar
Genevieve and Ralph Aguilar
Salome Alcantra*
John Allen
Brian Billy
Glen Billy
Matthew and Angelina Billy and children
Maude Billy
Dexter and Patty Bird
Virginia Knight Buck
Ethel Knight Burke*
Annabelle Campbell
Karen Casillas
Myrtle McKay Chavez
Lois Lockart Compton
Carmen Christy
Evangeline Duncan
Bonnie Elliott
Sharon Gonzalez
Edna Guerrero*
Delvin Holder
Sharon Allen Ibarra
Edgar and Pearl Jackson
Robert Jackson and family
Lenette Laiwa
Linda Aguilar McGill
Dorene Scott Mitchell
Emma Mitchell

Shirley Murguia
Keith Pike
Esther Ramirez
John Santana
Charlene Somersal
Laura Somersal*
Madeline Billy Thoeni
Victoria Reeves Walker
Marion Wilder
Brian Williams
Gayle Zepeda

Individual Support

Kat Anderson
Billie Ashiku
Jean Beaman
Alexis Canillo
Jerry Daviee
Jacqueline B. Dial
C.R. "Bob" Fairbairn
Lynn Fox
Peter Graves
Michael Harrison
Candace Horsley
Char Jacobs
Evan Johnson
Naomi Lane
Thomas N. Layton
Gaye LeBaron
Tom Liden
David Ludwig

James Maas
Tom Neil
Judith Polanich
Violet Renick
Maria Sakovich
Dan Shay
Sue Scammon
Kathleen Smith
Hank Steinbach
Marion Steinbach*
Mozelle Strickland
Hans Peter Thoeni
Kim Walters

*now deceased

Institutional Support

California State Library
Huntington Library
Jesse Peter Native American Art Museum
Lake County Library
Mendocino County Library
Mendocino County Museum
National Archives-Pacific Sierra Region
News from Native California
North Lake Tahoe Historical Society's
  Marion Steinbach Indian Basket Museum
Southwest Museum Library
Ukiah Daily Journal
U. S. Army Corps of Engineers

Pomo families gather for a photograph outside St. Mary's Church in Ukiah, c.1923.
Five weavers whose work is part of the Elsie Allen Collection appear in this image:
Annie Burke, Ethel Burke, Rhoda Knight, Elsie Allen, and Mollie Jackson. Many of
the others pictured are their relations including husbands, children, parents, siblings,
and cousins. Bernard Saunders, photographer

1.	Richard Burke	19.	Catherine Hansen	34.	Genevieve Allen (Aguilar)	54.	Margaret Mitchell
2.	Arthur Knight	20.	Kate Hansen Fred	35.	Lena Cordova Abasolo	56.	Blanche Knight Hermisillo
3.	Arthur Allen	21.	Charlie Wathan	36.	Catherine Williams	59.	Margaret Hansen
4.	Bill Graves	22.	Elmer Marando	40.	Myrtle Billy	60.	Tudy Marie Arnold
5.	Joe Myers	23.	Dennison "Bill" Knight	41.	Father Sebastian	61.	Rayfield Elliott
7.	Ed Beefe	24.	Fleming Knight	42.	Josephine Luff	62.	Marion Wilder Edwards
9.	Elsie Comanche Allen	25.	Angelo Knight	43.	Grace Williams	68.	Maude Knight
10.	Dick Reddick	26.	Louis Arnold	46.	Ruby Feliz	69.	Mollie Wright Jackson
11.	Salvador Burke	27.	Edgar Jackson	47.	Mandy Knight Feliz	72.	Sister Benedicta
13.	Jeff Joaquin	28.	Thomas Jackson	48.	Florence Hansen	74.	Gus Hughes
14.	Oscar Daniels	29.	Frederick Jackson	49.	Vernetta Lake	76.	Annie McWhinney
15.	Eva Fred	30.	Johnny Sherwood	50.	Nellie White	78.	Frank Miller
17.	Archie McWhinney	31.	Francis Allen	51.	Rhoda Somersal Knight	79.	Annie Ramon Burke
18.	John McWhinney	32.	Matthew Billy	52.	Ethel Knight Burke		
		33.	Catherine Billy	53.	Ada Mitchell		

Friends of *Remember Your Relations*

Major Donors

Suzanne Abel-Vidor
David & Margaret Alexander
James & Virginia Alexander
Leonard D. Allen
Verle Anderson
William K. & Stew Baker
Dr. & Mrs. Stuart Barton
Craig Bates
Laurence L. & Beth Belanger
Nancy Biggins
Glen Billy
Maude S. Billy
Susan Billy
Bo Ca Ama Council
Marge Boynton
Dot Brovarney
California Indian Basketweavers Association
Alexis Canillo
Nansi E. Corson
Lyn Dearborn
Stewart & Naomi Lynn Fox
Gloria Duffy
Barbara J. Goldeen & John R. Selmer
Peter Graves

Ruth Greenberg
Miriam Gruver & White Wolf
Jayne Harrah
Candace Horsley
Ira Jacknis
Ernest & Clara Lauteren
Rudy & Linda Light
Jackie Lowe
Dennis C.B. McDaniel
Suzanne A. McMeans
Dorene Mitchell
Lawrence G. Mondschein
Beverly R. Ortiz
Dr. & Mrs. John Pattee
David Rapport
Carol Rector
Jim Schee
Dorothy Sugawara
Alex R. & Mary Leittem Thomas
Fred H. Vann
Coosje van Bruggen
Karen P. Wehrman
Katherine W. Wilson
Barbara J. Winther

Donors

Bruce & Francine Bearden
Jane Bendix
Star Carroll-Smith
Marguerite Crown
Peter Elias and Mary Williams
Kathy Feigel
Dorothy B. Hunt
Ronald P. Koch

Thomas N. Layton
Jeannie MacGregor
Jo A. McMorris
George Morstyn
Jean Palmer
Adina W. Robinson
Wilda Schock
Madeline Thoeni